BY THE EDITORS OF

CONSUMER GUIDE®

Clay
Cookery

PUBLICATIONS INTERNATIONAL, LTD.

Contents

Front cover photography by Sacco Productions Limited/Chicago. Remaining photography by Dave Jordano Photography Inc.

Pictured on the front cover (clockwise from top left): Braided Egg Bread (page 127), Ginger Glazed Carrots (page 108), Cream Glazed Green Beans (page 106), Spanish Chicken with Rice (page 68) and Carrot Pineapple Cake (page 144).

Pictured on the back cover (top to bottom): Beef Stew with Vegetables (page 112) and Cherry Almond Ribbon Coffeecake (page 130).

Manufactured in Yugoslavia.

8 7 6 5 4 3 2

Introduction

At first glance a clay cooker appears to be an especially handsome casserole dish. However, anyone who has ever used this versatile cooking utensil knows that it is much, much more. A clay cooker comes as close as any one thing can to that magic pot of every cook's fantasies—a single vessel that can serve as, a soup kettle, a roaster for meat and poultry, a stew pot, a meat loaf pan, a fish poacher, a vegetable steamer, an all-purpose container for microwave cooking, a deep-dish pie pan, a soufflé dish and even as a little "brick oven" for the crustiest bread imaginable!

Sound impossible? Not when you know how to use a clay cooker to get the most out of its capabilities. That is what this book is about. The wide variety of recipes will acquaint you with the full potential of using a clay cooker, easily, neatly and all in your oven.

The important difference between a clay cooker and an ordinary casserole dish is that the cooker is unglazed, made of a special porous clay that is meant to be soaked and used *wet*. These rustic looking terra cotta cookers are designed to do their best work in a relatively hot oven.

You will find that cookers are available in many sizes and shapes. Some are designed for a single purpose, such as cooking a whole chicken or fish. But the most versatile are rectangular in shape with a high, domed cover that allows you to cook something as bulky as a ham or a stew made from bony meats. A useful size for beginning your adventures in clay cooking is a 3¼-quart (3.25 L) clay cooker. For party stews to serve a crowd or for a holiday turkey, you might like a larger one; for vegetables and side dishes, desserts or dishes for two, one of lesser capacity. (In this book, the given size of a clay cooker refers to the level volume that the lower portion of the cooker holds.)

Once you have a clay cooker, what can you expect from the food you cook in it? Wonderful flavor, for one important thing. Our ancient ancestors must have learned this when they selected various ceramic materials for their cooking pots, and it is still true: cooking in clay seems to keep natural flavors in, enriching and preserving them.

Soak the clay cooker in water to cover for about 15 minutes before placing food in the cooker.

How to Use a Clay Cooker

Most of the recipes in this book direct you to soak the clay cooker—top and bottom—in water to cover for about 15 minutes before adding food. As the cooker soaks, it absorbs a certain amount of water. Then, when the heat of the oven reaches the clay cooker, it heats this water first, causing an almost immediate flush of steam that begins heating the food to be cooked. Use your clay cooker *only* in the oven—never on top of the range.

There are some exceptions, but generally foods prepared in a clay cooker are baked in a fairly hot oven, 400°F (200°C) or hotter. With good planning, and especially if you have more than one clay cooker, you can cook two or more dishes in your oven at the same time to make the major portion of a meal.

The food in a clay cooker is covered throughout most of its baking time. This keeps moistness and flavor in and, as an added bonus, your oven remains relatively clean and unspattered. Occasionally, you will finish cooking a dish uncovered to give it a crispy brown color—but more often than not, attractive browning takes place while the food is covered. Examples of this are well browned, crusty soufflés and breads.

The browning capability of the clay cooker is one of its most appealing characteristics. Meats and poultry, particularly, brown beautifully when baked in the covered clay cooker. Even cut-up meats and chicken brown nicely, all in one baking operation. For most dishes, there is no need to brown food in added fat in a separate range-top step. As the meat bakes in the clay cooker, you may wish to stir or rearrange pieces once or twice so that all will brown well (recipes indicate when this is necessary).

After you have tried a variety of the recipes in this book, you will probably wonder how to go about converting some of your own favorite dishes so that they can benefit from clay cooking. Look at a similar clay cooker recipe and study its techniques. A rule-of-thumb for time and temperature conversions is to add 100°F (40°C) to the baking temperature and to increase the cooking time by about 30 minutes. (When baking poultry, however, cooking time will probably not be increased; in fact, cooking a whole chicken or turkey may take less time in a clay cooker.) Naturally, on a first attempt with any recipe, you should begin checking for doneness *well* in advance of the projected finishing point.

A clay cooker with a 3- to 3 1/2-quart (3 to 3.5 L) capacity is large enough for most of the recipes in this book. Some party-sized stews call for a larger one; if you have only the 3-quart (3 L) cooker, such recipes can be divided in half successfully. In such cases, baking times will be decreased also—start checking for doneness at least 45 minutes ahead of the time specified in the recipe.

Sometimes the size and shape of the clay cooker called for in a recipe is dictated by the food: for example, a plump breasted turkey necessitates using a clay cooker with a high domed cover. For a meat loaf or a loaf of bread of conventional shape, you will want a small loaf-shaped clay cooker. A large whole fish needs a long, narrow clay cooker—although you can cut the fish in half or into steaks and cook it in a shorter one, as well, decreasing the baking time as necessary.

If you use a smaller clay cooker than a recipe calls for, especially for a soup or stew, be sure you do not use excessive liquid. Otherwise, as the dish bakes and bubbles, liquid may boil over into your oven. When in doubt, use only part of the liquid, reserving the rest to add toward the end of the baking time, if it is needed.

Clay cookers can be used in both conventional and microwave ovens. Many people find a clay cooker ideally suited to microwave cooking of less tender cuts of meat, feeling that the cooker contributes to browning and tenderizing.

To make the most of this effect, you need a microwave oven with variable power settings so that such meats can be cooked at a lower power setting (medium-low or simmer). Even in a clay cooker, only tender meats should be cooked at full power. Poultry, fish, vegetables, desserts, and the like can be cooked in a clay cooker at standard full power in any microwave oven. The microwave oven recipes in this cookbook were designed especially for clay cooking; if you want to try another dish, check the power setting specified in a similar recipe to guide your time and power choices.

Taking Care of Your Clay Cooker

Before using a new clay cooker for the first time, soak the top and bottom in water to cover them for about half an hour. Then scrub all surfaces well with a brush to remove any clay dust. Now the cooker is soaked and ready to use.

A clay cooker is vulnerable to sudden temperature changes, so it is *always* essential to begin baking in a cold oven. That way, the cooker and the oven heat up gradually at the same time. A

Use thick potholders when removing clay cooker from the oven; place hot cooker on thick cork or wooden board.

A stiff brush or a plastic scouring pad is very useful for cleaning your clay cooker.

When storing your clay cooker, place the bottom of the cooker inside the inverted cover.

rapid change in temperature may cause the cooker to crack or break. Remember this principle also when you handle the clay cooker; it is just as important when you remove the hot cooker from the oven. (Be sure to provide yourself with good thick potholders, a must for handling a clay cooker sizzling hot from the oven.) Place the cooker on a thick cork, straw or fabric mat or a wooden board; never put it on a cold surface.

In some recipes in this cookbook, you will begin with part of the ingredients and cook them to a certain stage; then you'll remove the clay cooker from the oven to add other ingredients. Make the additions in a reasonable amount of time so that the clay cooker is still rather warm to the touch when you return it to the hot oven. Also, when adding ingredients to a hot clay cooker, the added ingredients should not be refrigerator-cold. Let the empty clay cooker cool to room temperature before adding water to soak away cooked-on food.

With use, both top and bottom of a clay cooker change color. Many people feel this adds to their homey, rustic quality. Cooked-on food is another story. A clay cooker should not be washed in the dishwasher; harsh dishwasher chemicals can affect food flavors, and too many changes of temperature are involved.

Wash your clay cooker in warm water using just a *few drops* of gentle dishwashing liquid. Let it soak for a few minutes to loosen dirt. If a stiff brush or a plastic scouring pad (do not use soap-filled metal pads) won't finish the job, let the cooker soak overnight filled with water and 1 to 4 tablespoons (15 to 60 mL) of baking soda. This will also help to freshen the clay pot when you have used it for pungent tasting foods.

Be sure your clay cooker is completely dry before storing it. Place the bottom of the cooker so that it rests lightly inside the inverted cover. Thus, the inside of the lower portion will be exposed to the air. If you live in a damp or muggy climate and your clay cooker remains unused for long periods of time, you may find that spots of mold appear during storage. If this should happen, brush the surface with a paste made with equal parts of baking soda and water. Let stand for 30 minutes, then brush away, rinse well and let the clay cooker dry where there is good air circulation, if possible in bright sunlight.

One way to keep your clay cooker free of cooking stains is to line it with baking parchment paper before adding food. This isn't necessary, but in this book we recommend it when certain foods such as fish and shellfish, strong flavored vegetables or large quantities of garlic are involved. This prevents these vigorous flavors from being retained in the pores of the clay to reappear where they might not be wanted. After all, you wouldn't like your blueberry dessert to taste like Shrimp de Jonghe. When the use of parchment paper is specified in a recipe, one of two directions is given. "Line the bottom and sides of cooker" means to line the entire bottom portion of the cooker. "Line cooker with parchment paper cut to fit bottom only" means to line the flat (or ridged) base of the lower portion of the cooker. The cover or top portion of the cooker is never lined with paper.

Handle your clay cooker with care and it should give you hundreds of delicious dishes; but, if one should chip or break, it can be mended. Look for a glue that can withstand the high oven temperatures used for clay cookery. Clear silicone glue in a tube, used according to the manufacturer's directions, is good for repairs when necessary.

Cooking with Metrics

You should become acquainted with metric measurements, since they will soon be adopted universally. All of our recipes provide easy lessons. Every measurement is given in the units we are accustomed to, as well as in metric equivalents. Also, temperatures are given in both Fahrenheit and Celsius degrees. These equivalents are rounded off to the nearest convenient metric measurements. Thus, although not exact conversions, the *proportion* of ingredients remains the same. Common metric abbreviations are: mL=millilitre; L=litre (1000 millilitres); g=gram; kg=kilogram (1000 grams); and cm=centimetre.

An easy method to use to "line cooker with parchment paper cut to fit bottom only" is to place the bottom of the cooker on paper, draw a line around the base, and then cut the parchment on the line you have drawn.

To "line the bottom and sides of cooker," place parchment paper in entire bottom portion of cooker.

Savory Soups with Wonderful Rich Flavors

Soup from oven? As you discover the versatility of your clay cooker, you won't be surprised to learn that it can produce some of the most richly flavored soups you have ever tasted.

Be sure to use a clay cooker large enough to hold the soup. Measure the capacity of the bottom section to be sure it will accommodate all the soup without bubbling over in your oven. Each recipe in this chapter specifies a clay cooker of sufficient size. In making a clay cooker soup, the size of such ingredients as vegetables and bony meats may vary somewhat. If you see that your clay cooker seems overfull, add liquid only to within about one inch of the top before cooking—reserve any remaining liquid and add it near the end of the cooking time.

When you cook a fish soup in clay, such as the Creamy Seafood Chowder or the Basque Fisherman's Soup, it is a good idea to line the soaked clay cooker with baking parchment paper. This will keep fishy flavors from carrying over into the next food you prepare in the cooker.

When you cook hearty soups made with beans, lentils and other foods that benefit by longer, slower cooking, the oven temperature for cooking these soups in clay can be somewhat lower than for meats. Soups made with fresh vegetables, fish and quick-cooking meats, on the other hand, will be ready in a jiffy in your clay cooker in a 400° to 450°F (200° to 230°C) oven.

Take advantage of the oven in which your clay cooker soup is bubbling. Use it for accompaniments: most brown-and-serve breads bake in a 450°F (230°C) oven, and a slightly lower oven temperature can be used for homemade yeast breads and quick breads. In the chapter entitled "Desserts to Serve Temptingly Warm," you will find recipes for several hot fruit dishes and homey puddings that are just right for putting a finishing touch to a satisfying soup supper.

A handsome clay cooker makes a good serving dish for soup —you can bring it to the table straight from the oven. Remember that the clay cooker will be very hot! Use a sturdy trivet of cork or wood to protect your table. In a covered clay cooker, soup stays steaming hot and ready for second servings for up to an hour.

Oven Onion Soup

Makes 6 servings

6 large onions, thinly sliced
2 cloves garlic, minced
2 tablespoons (30 mL) butter or margarine
1/4 teaspoon (1 mL) dried thyme leaves
3 cans (13 3/4 ounces or 400 g each) regular-strength or 5 1/4 cups (1310 mL) homemade beef broth
1 cup (250 mL) dry white wine
 Salt
 Freshly ground pepper
6 slices French bread, 1/2 inch (1.5 cm) thick
1 cup (250 mL) freshly grated Parmesan cheese
1 cup (250 mL) shredded aged Swiss cheese

Traditional French onion soup, laden with crisp slices of toast and crowned with melted cheese, is easy to prepare in a clay cooker.

1. Soak top and bottom of a 3 1/4-quart (3.25 L) clay cooker in water about 15 minutes; drain.

2. Place onions and garlic in cooker; dot with butter.

3. Place covered cooker in cold oven. Set oven at 400°F (200°C). Bake, stirring once or twice, until onions are limp and light brown, about 1 hour.

4. Sprinkle onions with thyme. Pour in broth and wine. Bake covered 1 hour. Season to taste with salt and pepper.

5. While soup is cooking, toast bread in oven until light brown, 15 to 20 minutes. Combine Parmesan and Swiss cheeses. Float toast slices in single layer over soup. Sprinkle evenly with cheeses.

6. Increase oven temperature to 450°F (230°C). Bake soup uncovered 10 minutes. Increase oven temperature to 550°F (290°C) and/or broil; cook until cheese is bubbling and golden, about 2 minutes. Serve very hot.

Creamy Seafood Chowder

Makes 3 to 4 servings

1 shallot, minced or 2 tablespoons (30 mL) minced onion
1 rib celery, finely chopped
2 tablespoons (30 mL) butter or margarine
1/2 pound (225 g) raw shrimp, shelled, deveined
1 jar (10 ounces or 285 g) or 1 1/4 cups (310 mL) small to medium oysters, undrained
1 bay leaf
1 cup (250 mL) whipping cream
1 can (13 3/4 ounces or 400 g) regular-strength or 1 3/4 cups (430 mL) homemade chicken broth
1/2 cup (125 mL) dry white wine
 Salt
 White pepper
2 tablespoons (30 mL) minced fresh parsley

This elegant soup is a rich combination of shrimp and oysters in a creamy broth laced with white wine. Offer it as a first course, or serve it to two or three seafood enthusiasts as a main course, accompanied by hot buttered French bread toast.

1. Soak top and bottom of 2-quart (2 L) clay cooker in water about 15 minutes; drain. Line bottom and sides of cooker with parchment paper.

2. Combine shallot and celery in cooker; dot with butter.

3. Place covered cooker in cold oven. Set oven at 400°F (200°C). Bake, stirring once or twice, until vegetables are limp, about 25 minutes.

4. Place shrimp, oysters with liquid and bay leaf over vegetables. Pour in cream. Stir in broth and wine gradually. Bake covered until shrimp are pink and oysters are opaque, 30 to 40 minutes.

5. Taste soup and add salt and pepper, if needed. Remove bay leaf. Stir in parsley. Serve immediately.

Herbed Zucchini Soup

Makes 6 servings

4   Slices bacon, coarsely chopped
6   to 8 medium zucchini (about 2½ pounds or 1125 g), cut into ½-inch (1.5 cm) slices
1   medium onion, chopped
1   small clove garlic, cut into slivers
1   can (10½ ounces or 300 g) condensed or 1¼ cups (310 mL) homemade beef broth
2½ cups (625 mL) water
¼ cup (60 mL) minced fresh parsley
1   teaspoon (5 mL) dried basil leaves
1   teaspoon (5 mL) salt
⅛ teaspoon (0.5 mL) pepper
    Grated Parmesan cheese

Good for a sipping soup in mugs as a first course, or for a satisfying lunch with grilled sandwiches, this zucchini soup is smoothly puréed. It freezes well if the recipe makes more than you need.

1. Soak top and bottom of 3¼-quart (3.25 mL) clay cooker in water about 15 minutes; drain.

2. Place bacon pieces in cooker.

3. Place covered cooker in cold oven. Set oven at 450°F (230°C). Bake, stirring once or twice, until bacon is light brown, 20 to 25 minutes. Pour off and discard drippings.

4. Add remaining ingredients except cheese.

5. Reduce oven temperature to 400°F (200°C). Bake covered until zucchini is tender, about 40 minutes.

6. Process mixture, about 2 cups (500 mL) at a time, in blender or food processor until smooth. Return mixture to cooker; bake covered until very hot, about 10 minutes. Serve with cheese to sprinkle over each serving.

Moroccan Lentil Soup

Makes 4 to 6 servings

1½ cups (375 mL) dried lentils, rinsed, drained
1   lamb shank (about 1 pound or 450 g)
1   can (1 pound or 450 g) tomatoes, coarsely chopped, liquid reserved
1   large onion, chopped
2   cloves garlic, minced
1½ teaspoons (7 mL) salt
¾ teaspoon (4 mL) ground coriander
½ teaspoon (2 mL) ground cumin
½ teaspoon (2 mL) ground turmeric
1   dried small hot red pepper, crushed
4   to 5 cups (1 L to 1250 mL) water
¼ cup (60 mL) minced fresh parsley
    Lemon wedges

North African restaurants serve a similar spicy soup as one of the early dishes in a multi-course menu. It is good that way, or as the featured dish of a family soup supper with crisp flat bread or bread sticks and raw vegetable relishes.

1. Soak top and bottom of 3¼-quart (3.25 L) clay cooker in water about 15 minutes; drain.

2. Combine lentils, lamb shank and tomatoes with reserved liquid in cooker. Add onion, garlic, salt, spices and red pepper. Pour in 4 cups (1 L) water.

3. Place covered cooker in cold oven. Set oven at 375°F (190°C). Bake, stirring once or twice, until lentils and lamb are very tender, 2½ to 3 hours.

4. Remove lamb shank from soup; cover soup and return to oven. When shank is cool enough to handle, discard bones, fat and skin, cut meat into bite-size pieces. Return meat to soup. Taste and add more salt, if needed. If soup is too thick, add up to 1 cup (250 mL) water.

5. Bake covered 15 minutes. Stir in parsley. Serve very hot with lemon wedges.

Black Bean and Sausage Soup

Makes 4 to 6 servings

1   **pound (450 g) or about 2 cups (500 mL) dried black beans, rinsed, drained**
7   **to 7¹/₂ cups (1750 mL to 1875 mL) water**
2   **ribs celery with leaves, finely chopped**
2   **medium onions, chopped**
3   **cloves garlic, minced**
1   **dried small hot red pepper, crushed**
2   **teaspoons (10 mL) salt**
1   **teaspoon (5 mL) ground coriander**
¹/₄   **teaspoon (1 mL) ground cloves**
1¹/₂   **pounds (675 g) Polish sausage or smoked bratwurst, cut into 1-inch (2.5 cm) pieces**
   Sour cream

Black beans cook to a unique color, a sort of deep purple-brown. Their flavor in this main dish soup with chunks of smoked sausage is special, too. In Cuba, black bean soup is served with bowls of rice and raw onion, to be mixed in at the table. This version calls for a dollop of sour cream over each serving — a cool contrast to the steaming beans.

1. Place beans in a large bowl; add 4 cups (1 L) of the water. Let stand overnight. [Or, heat beans and 4 cups (1 L) water in 4-quart (4 L) kettle to boiling; boil briskly 2 minutes; remove from heat. Let stand covered 1 hour.] Do not drain beans.

2. Soak top and bottom of 3¹/₄-quart (3.25 L) clay cooker in water about 15 minutes; drain.

3. Combine beans and their liquid, 3 more cups (750 mL) water and the remaining ingredients except sausage and sour cream in cooker.

4. Place covered cooker in cold oven. Set oven at 375°F (190°C). Bake, stirring once or twice, until beans are nearly tender, about 2¹/₂ hours.

5. Mash beans slightly; stir in sausage and up to ¹/₂ cup (125 mL) more water, if soup is too thick. Bake covered until beans are very tender, about 1 hour. Taste and add more salt, if needed. Serve with dollops of sour cream.

Old-Fashioned Ham and Bean Soup

Makes 4 to 6 servings

1   **pound (450 g) or about 2 cups (500 mL) dried Great Northern beans, rinsed, drained**
8   **cups (2 L) water**
2   **smoked ham hocks (about 2 pounds or 900 g)**
1   **rib celery with leaves, finely chopped**
1   **large onion, chopped**
¹/₄   **cup (60 mL) minced fresh parsley**
¹/₂   **teaspoon (2 mL) dried marjoram leaves**
¹/₈   **teaspoon (0.5 mL) ground cloves**
1   **bay leaf**
   Salt
   White Pepper

This soup is enriched with the flavor of smoked ham hocks. They are first cooked with the beans, then later cut into bite-size pieces and returned to the soup to make a meaty main course. Serve the soup with warm corn bread and a tart coleslaw.

1. Place beans in large bowl; add 4 cups (1 L) of the water. Let stand overnight. [Or, heat beans and 4 cups (1 L) water in 4-quart (4 L) kettle to boiling; boil briskly 2 minutes; remove from heat. Let stand covered 1 hour.] Do not drain beans.

2. Soak top and bottom of 3¹/₄-quart (3.25 L) clay cooker in water about 15 minutes; drain.

3. Combine beans and their liquid, 2 more cups (500 mL) of the water and remaining ingredients except salt and pepper in cooker.

4. Place covered cooker in cold oven. Set oven at 375°F (190°C). Bake, stirring once or twice, until beans and ham are very tender, 3 to 3¹/₂ hours.
(Continued on page 16)

OLD-FASHIONED HAM AND BEAN SOUP, continued

5. Remove ham hocks from soup. Mash beans slightly; stir in remaining 2 cups water. Cover soup and return to oven. When ham hocks are cool enough to handle, discard bones, fat and skin; cut meat into bite-size pieces. Return meat to soup. Remove bay leaf. Taste and add salt and pepper, if needed.

6. Bake covered 30 minutes. Serve very hot.

Leek and Potato Soup

Makes 6 to 8 servings

6	**to 8 leeks**
3	**tablespoons (45 mL) butter or margarine**
¹/₃	**cup (80 mL) minced fresh parsley**
4	**medium boiling potatoes, pared, cut into ¹/₂-inch (1.5 cm) cubes (about 3 cups or 750 mL)**
1	**large can (47 ounces or 1125 g) or 6 cups (1.5 L) homemade chicken broth**
	Salt
	White pepper

Here is another favorite French soup. Leeks are expensive, but so flavorful they are worth their price. Look for them in supermarkets that specialize in good produce.

1. Soak top and bottom of 3¹/₄-quart (3.25 L) clay cooker in water about 15 minutes; drain.

2. Trim off root ends of leeks. To clean, slit leeks from bottoms and rinse well to remove grit. Cut leeks into slices, using about half the green tops. Place leeks in cooker; dot with butter.

3. Place covered cooker in cold oven. Set oven at 400°F (200°C). Bake, stirring once or twice, until leeks are limp but not brown, about 40 minutes.

4. Add parsley, potatoes and 4 cups (1 L) of the chicken broth. Bake covered until potatoes are very tender, about 1 hour.

5. Process mixture, about 2 cups (500 mL) at a time, in blender or food processor until smooth. Return mixture to cooker; stir in remaining chicken broth. Bake covered until very hot, about 10 minutes. Season to taste with salt and pepper. Serve immediately.

Mulligatawny

Makes 4 to 5 servings

1	**large frying chicken (3¹/₂ to 4 pounds or 1500 to 1800 g), cut up**
1	**dried small hot red pepper, crushed**
1	**tablespoon (15 mL) ground coriander**
2	**teaspoons (10 mL) ground turmeric**

The unusual name of this golden chicken soup is taken from a southern Indian dialect word meaning "pepper water." Peppery it is, but only mildly so with the heat of a small dried red chile. Other exotic spices combine to give the soup a curry flavor. Accompany it with a cucumber salad and thinly sliced whole wheat bread.

1. Soak top and bottom of 3¹/₄-quart (3.25 mL) clay cooker in water about 15 minutes; drain.

MULLIGATAWNY, continued

1¹/₂   teaspoons (7 mL) salt
¹/₄   teaspoon (1 mL) whole cloves
¹/₄   teaspoon (1 mL) ground ginger
2   medium onions, thinly sliced
2   cloves garlic, minced
5   cups (1250 mL) water
1   can (15 ounces or 425 g) garbanzo beans, drained
     Lemon wedges
     Toasted grated unsweetened coconut*
     Plain yogurt

2. Place chicken pieces in clay cooker. Sprinkle with mixture of red pepper, coriander, turmeric, salt, cloves and ginger. Top with onions and garlic. Pour in 4 cups (1 L) of the water.

3. Place covered cooker in cold oven. Set oven at 400°F (200°C). Bake until chicken is very tender, 2¹/₂ to 3 hours.

4. Remove chicken pieces from soup. Stir garbanzo beans into broth, partially mashing them with fork to thicken soup. Cover soup and return to oven. When chicken pieces are cool enough to handle, discard bones and skin; cut meat into generous bite-size pieces. Return meat to soup. Stir in remaining 1 cup (250 mL) water.

5. Reduce oven temperature to 350°F (180°C). Bake soup covered 30 minutes. Serve with lemon wedges, coconut and yogurt.

NOTE: *To toast coconut, bake in shallow pan at 400°F (200°C) stirring 2 to 3 times with fork, until lightly browned, 5 to 8 minutes.

Makes 6 servings

Basque Fisherman's Soup

1   medium onion, sliced
1   clove garlic, minced
1   small red or green pepper, finely chopped
1   rib celery, finely chopped
1   pound (450 g) fish fillets, thawed if frozen, cut into bite-size pieces
1   can (10 ounces or 285 g) small whole clams, undrained
¹/₄   pound (115 g) shelled, cooked small deveined shrimp
¹/₂   teaspoon (2 mL) Italian herb seasoning
¹/₈   teaspoon (0.5 mL) cayenne pepper
2   tablespoons (30 mL) tomato paste
1   can (10³/₄ ounces or 310 g) condensed tomato soup
1¹/₄   cups (310 mL) warm water
¹/₂   cup (125 mL) dry white wine
2   tablespoons (30 mL) minced fresh parsley

This simple soup combines readily available fish and shellfish. Choose any favorite fresh or frozen fish — turbot, haddock, cod, perch or sole — and combine it with clams and shrimp in a tomato-flavored broth sparked with a dash of cayenne. Ladled over hot buttery garlic toast in warm bowls, and served with a light red wine, this hearty soup will take the chill off the coldest evening.

1. Soak top and bottom of 3¹/₄-quart (3.25 L) clay cooker in water about 15 minutes; drain. Line bottom and side of cooker with parchment paper.

2. Combine onion, garlic, red pepper and celery in cooker. Top with fish, clams with liquid and shrimp. Sprinkle with herb seasoning and cayenne. Mix tomato paste and soup in medium bowl. Stir in warm water gradually; stir in wine. Pour mixture over fish.

3. Place covered cooker in cold oven. Set oven at 400°F. (200°C). Bake, stirring once or twice, until vegetables are crisp-tender, 1¹/₄ to 1¹/₂ hours. Stir in parsley. Serve immediately.

Cooking Meats for Tenderness and Variety

Good cooks have always looked for ways to cook meat to perfection—good tasting, juicy, tender. Baking meat in clay is one of the oldest methods and still one of the best.

You can use your clay cooker to prepare meat in just about any style: a crusty beef roast that is rare in the center, a fork-tender pot roast with vegetables, a classic country stew, a favorite family meat loaf or an elegant main dish of French or Italian origin. Cooking in clay is versatile, indeed!

One of the greatest benefits is the flavor of the meat. When you cook in a clay pot, the cover stays on, keeping the aromatic components of meat and seasonings inside to mingle and penetrate. Covered cooking in clay also results in moist, tender meat, whether you cook a beef or lamb roast just long enough for a rare interior, or use the moist heat of the clay cooker for a longer time to stew or braise less tender meats.

This style of meat cooking is a remarkably simple one. Meats rarely require browning on top of the range. The clay cooker does it all in the oven, with just an occasional stir to redistribute meat that is in small pieces. This means you can cook without adding fat, and it also saves on dishwashing and kitchen clean-up.

Porous clay cookers can absorb flavors just as they absorb liquid. When you prepare meat with pungent ingredients, such as garlic, vinegar, sauerkraut and cabbage, you may wish to line the clay cooker with cooking parchment paper to prevent their flavors from carrying over.

When you prepare a roast in a clay cooker an important adjunct is a meat thermometer. Baking times given in recipes can only approximate the time it takes for a beef or lamb roast of a specific weight and shape to reach just the stage of doneness you prefer. It is also a must when cooking a pork roast to be sure the inside temperature reaches the point that meat experts consider safe. Insert the thermometer in the thickest part of the meat, positioned at an angle so that the cover of the clay cooker will clear it. If the roast stands for five to ten minutes before carving, you can turn off the oven when the internal temperature is about 5°F (3°C) below the desired temperature; the heat retained inside the cooker will continue cooking the meat.

Sirloin Tip Roast with Green Peppercorns

2   tablespoons (30 mL) canned or 1 tablespoon (15 mL) freeze-dried green peppercorns, rinsed, drained

2   tablespoons (30 mL) butter or margarine, room temperature

1   clove garlic, minced

1 1/2   teaspoons (7 mL) Dijon-style mustard

1/8   teaspoon (0.5 mL) dried tarragon leaves

1   rolled boneless sirloin tip roast (4 1/2 to 5 pounds or 2 kg to 2250 g)

1/4   cup (60 mL) brandy

1/2   cup (125 mL) whipping cream

Green peppercorns or poivre vert *are an elegant new seasoning used in French cooking to flavor a range of foods, from steaks to duckling. Here they season a delicious rolled, boneless beef roast and its sauce. Look for the peppercorns, which are the tender, immature version of black pepper, canned in brine or freeze-dried in gourmet shops.*

1. Soak top and bottom of 3 1/4-quart (3.25 L) clay cooker in water about 15 minutes; drain.

2. While cooker is soaking, crush green peppercorns slightly with a fork in small bowl. Stir in butter, garlic, mustard and tarragon. Spread butter mixture on all sides of roast. Place roast, fat side up, in cooker. Pour in brandy. Insert meat thermometer in thickest part of roast.

3. Place covered cooker in cold oven. Set oven at 425°F (220°C). Bake until meat is about 5°F (3°C) below desired temperature [135°F (57°C) for rare, 145°F (63°C) for medium-rare to medium], 1 1/2 to 2 hours. Remove cover; bake until meat is brown, 5 to 10 minutes.

4. Pour off cooking liquid. Cover cooker to keep meat warm. Skim and discard fat from cooking liquid. Pour liquid into skillet; stir in cream. Heat to boiling; cook, stirring occasionally until reduced by about half.

5. Carve roast; pour sauce over slices.

Boeuf à la Mode

1   boneless rump or bottom round roast (4 pounds or 1800 g)

1/4   cup (60 mL) brandy

1 1/2   cups (375 mL) dry red wine

1   medium onion, thinly sliced, separated into rings

1   clove garlic, minced

1   teaspoon (5 mL) salt

1/4   teaspoon (1 mL) black peppercorns

1/4   teaspoon (1 mL) dried thyme leaves

1/8   teaspoon (0.5 mL) ground nutmeg

Here is a classic French pot roast — marinated in herbs, garlic and red wine, then oven-braised flavorfully with new potatoes and carrots. You will find that even a compact, less tender beef roast becomes fork-tender thanks to gentle clay cooking.

1. Place meat in deep bowl. Pour in brandy and wine. Add onion, garlic, salt, peppercorns, thyme, nutmeg, cloves and bay leaf; turn roast with herbs to combine ingredients. Refrigerate covered 8 hours or overnight.

2. Soak top and bottom of 3 1/4-quart (3.25 L) clay cooker in water about 15 minutes; drain.

3. Place roast, fat side up, in cooker; pour marinade and beef broth over roast.

BOEUF À LA MODE, continued

1/8 teaspoon (0.5 mL) whole cloves
1 bay leaf
1 cup (250 mL) regular-strength beef broth, canned or homemade
6 small new potatoes, scrubbed
6 medium carrots, pared
2 teaspoons (10 mL) flour
1 tablespoon (15 mL) butter or margarine, room temperature
  Minced fresh parsley

4. Place covered cooker in cold oven. Set oven at 425°F (220°C). Bake 2 hours.

5. While roast is baking, pare 1-inch (2.5 cm) strip around center of each potato. Cut carrots lengthwise into quarters. Place carrots and potatoes around roast. Bake covered until meat and vegetables are tender, about 1 hour.

6. Remove meat and vegetables to warm serving platter; keep warm. Strain cooking liquid; skim and discard fat. Pour liquid into large skillet. Heat to boiling; cook, stirring occasionally, until reduced by about a third. Mix flour and butter; stir into liquid. Cook and stir until thickened and clear.

7. Carve roast; sprinkle parsley over vegetables; spoon sauce over meat and vegetables.

Makes 6 to 8 servings

Sauerbraten

2 1/2 cups (625 mL) Rhine wine
2 medium onions, thinly sliced
1 medium carrot, pared, thinly sliced
1 clove garlic, cut into slivers
1 bay leaf
1 1/2 tablespoons (22 mL) sugar
1 tablespoon (15 mL) mixed whole pickling spices
1 teaspoon (5 mL) whole cloves
1 teaspoon (5 mL) ground ginger
1/2 teaspoon (2 mL) black peppercorns
1/2 teaspoon (2 mL) dried thyme leaves
1/2 cup (125 mL) red wine vinegar
1 Boneless rump roast (4 1/2 to 5 pounds or 2 kg to 2250 g)
1 tablespoon (15 mL) tomato paste
2 teaspoons (10 mL) salt
1/3 cup (80 mL) dark raisins
1 tablespoon (15 mL) cornstarch
2 tablespoons (30 mL) water

The clay cooker really shines when you use if for less tender meats, such as the rump roast in this German favorite, spicy marinated Sauerbraten. With the sliced beef and shimmering sauce, serve noodles and the Old-Fashioned Spiced Applesauce (see Index for page number).

1. Two to four days before cooking beef, heat wine, onions, carrot, garlic, bay leaf, sugar, pickling spices, cloves, ginger, peppercorns and thyme just until about to boil. Remove from heat; stir in vinegar. Pour marinade over roast in deep bowl. Refrigerate covered, turning meat and stirring marinade occasionally, 2 to 4 days.

2. Soak top and bottom of 3 1/4-quart (3.25 L) clay cooker in water about 15 minutes; drain.

3. Place roast, fat side up, in cooker. Stir tomato paste and salt into marinade. Pour marinade over roast.

4. Place covered cooker in cold oven. Set oven at 425°F (220°C). Bake until meat is very tender, about 3 hours.

5. Pour off cooking liquid. Cover cooker to keep meat warm. Strain cooking liquid; skim and discard fat. Pour liquid into large skillet; stir in raisins. Heat to boiling; remove from heat. Mix cornstarch and water; stir into skillet. Cook, stirring constantly, until thickened and clear.

6. Carve roast; spoon sauce over slices.

German Stuffed Beef Rolls

2 pounds boneless top round, about 3/8 inch (1 cm) thick
Coarsely ground Dijon-style mustard
6 thin slices Black Forest or boiled ham
6 small sour pickles
Paprika
Flour
1 small onion, finely chopped
1 clove garlic, minced
3/4 cup (180 mL) regular-strength beef broth, canned or homemade
1/2 cup (125 mL) whipping cream
Minced fresh parsley

Inside each of these moist, tender little rolls of top round is a piquant stuffing, combining mustard, a sour pickle and a thin slice of ham. A creamy sauce adds finesse.

1. Soak top and bottom of 2-quart (2 L) clay cooker in water about 15 minutes; drain.

2. Meanwhile, cut beef into 6 equal pieces, trimming fat. Pound each piece between sheets of waxed paper, using flat side of meat mallet, until meat is less than 1/4 inch (0.5 cm) thick.

3. Spread each piece lightly with mustard; top with ham slice. Place pickle at one end of each piece of meat; tuck in sides and roll up firmly. Fasten ends with small metal skewers or tie firmly at each end with clean white string. Sprinkle meat rolls lightly with paprika; coat lightly with flour.

4. Place meat rolls in single layer in cooker. Sprinkle with onion and garlic. Pour in beef broth.

5. Place covered cooker in cold oven. Set oven at 425°F (220°C). Bake until meat is very tender, 2 to 2 1/2 hours.

6. Pour cooking liquid into medium skillet. Cover cooker to keep beef rolls warm. Stir cream into cooking liquid. Heat to boiling; cook, stirring constantly, until sauce thickens slightly. Pour sauce over beef rolls. Garnish with parsley.

Snappy Rice-Stuffed Meatballs

1 pound (450 g) ground lean beef
1/3 cup (80 mL) uncooked long-grain white rice
2 cups (500 mL) spicy-hot tomato juice cocktail
1 teaspoon (5 mL) salt
1 clove garlic, minced
1 small onion, thinly sliced, separated into rings
1 small green pepper, cut into thin strips

The flavor of these no-fuss meatballs comes from piquant canned tomato juice cocktail — the sort intended for making the drink called a Bloody Mary. Meatballs and sauce all cook in one easy oven procedure in just over an hour.

1. Soak top and bottom of 2-quart (2 L) clay cooker in water about 15 minutes; drain.

2. Combine ground beef, rice, 1/4 cup (60 mL) of the tomato juice and the salt; shape into 1-inch (2.5 cm) balls. Place in cooker; top with garlic, onion and green pepper. Pour in remaining tomato juice.

3. Place covered cooker in cold oven. Set oven at 450°F (230°C). Bake, stirring once or twice, until rice and vegetables are tender, about 1 hour 10 minutes.

Elegant Corned Beef

Makes 8 to 10 servings

1 corned beef brisket (4 to 5
 pounds or 1800 to 2250 g)
2 cups (500 mL) water
1 lemon
1/2 cup (125 mL) packed brown
 sugar
1/4 cup (60 mL) fine dry bread
 crumbs
1 teaspoon (5 mL) Dijon-style
 mustard
 Whole cloves
1/2 cup (125 mL) dry sherry

First oven-simmer corned beef in the clay cooker, then dress it up with a tart, lemony-sweet glaze for a party dish. The moist, tender, clove-studded meat slices well, and is ideal for a buffet.

1. Soak top and bottom of 3 1/4-quart (3.25 L) clay cooker in water about 15 minutes; drain.

2. Rinse corned beef with cold running water. Place corned beef in deep kettle; add water to cover. Heat to boiling; drain. Place corned beef, fat side up, in cooker; add 2 cups (500 mL) water.

3. Place covered cooker in cold oven. Set oven at 425°F (220°C). Bake until corned beef is tender, about 2 hours; pour off and discard cooking liquid.

4. While corned beef is baking, grate lemon rind; squeeze and reserve lemon juice. Mix brown sugar, bread crumbs, mustard and lemon rind. Stud top of corned beef with cloves; pat brown sugar mixture over top of brisket. Mix lemon juice and sherry; drizzle half the mixture over corned beef.

5. Bake covered 30 minutes. Drizzle with remaining sherry mixture. Bake uncovered until topping is browned, 10 to 15 minutes. Cut corned beef into thin slices; spoon cooking liquid over slices.

Ground Beef Parmentier

Makes 6 servings

4 medium boiling potatoes
 (about 2 pounds or 900 g),
 pared, cut into chunks
1 1/2 pounds (675 g) ground lean
 beef
1 small onion, finely chopped
1 clove garlic, minced
1 teaspoon (5 mL) red wine
 vinegar
1 teaspoon (5 mL) salt
1/8 teaspoon (0.5 mL) pepper
1/4 cup (60 mL) milk
2 tablespoons (30 mL) butter or
 margarine
1/8 teaspoon (0.5 mL) paprika
 Dash nutmeg
 Salt
1/2 cup (125 mL) shredded Swiss
 cheese

A puffy cheese-crusted potato pureé crowns this simple ground beef loaf. A platter of sliced tomatoes, drizzled with red wine vinegar and a few drops of oil and sprinkled with sliced green onions, makes a colorful side dish.

1. Cook potatoes in boiling salted water until tender, about 15 minutes; drain well.

2. Soak top and bottom of 2-quart (2 L) clay cooker in water about 15 minutes; drain.

3. Combine ground beef, onion, garlic, vinegar, 1 teaspoon (5 mL) salt and the pepper; spread in cooker.

4. Place potatoes, milk, butter, paprika and nutmeg in mixer bowl; beat until smooth. Season to taste with salt. Spread evenly over ground beef. Sprinkle with cheese.

5. Place covered cooker in cold oven. Set oven at 475°F (250°C). Bake until juices from meat are clear and edges are brown and crusty, 35 to 45 minutes. Remove cover; bake until top browns, 8 to 10 minutes.

Grecian Beef Stew

3	pounds (1350 g) boneless beef chuck, fat trimmed, cut into 1-inch (2.5 cm) cubes
1¹/2	tablespoons (22 mL) flour
1¹/2	teaspoons (7 mL) salt
¹/2	teaspoon (2 mL) ground cinnamon
2	teaspoons (10 mL) mixed whole pickling spices
3	cloves garlic, minced
2	tablespoons (30 mL) dark raisins
1	tablespoon (15 mL) brown sugar
2	small onions, each cut into 6 wedges
1	cup (250 mL) dry red wine
1	can (8 ounces or 225 g) tomato sauce
3	tablespoons (45 mL) red wine vinegar
	Minced fresh parsley

Cinnamon, brown sugar, raisins, red wine and vinegar give this Mediterranean main course a beguiling sweet-sour spiced flavor. For accompaniments, choose brown rice and a cucumber, lettuce and tomato salad.

1. Soak top and bottom of 3¹/4-quart (3.25 L) clay cooker in water about 15 minutes; drain.

2. Coat beef cubes with mixture of flour, salt and cinnamon. Place beef cubes in cooker. Tie pickling spices securely in cheesecloth; place in center of cooker. Sprinkle beef with garlic, raisins and brown sugar. Top with onions. Mix wine, tomato sauce and vinegar; pour into cooker.

3. Place covered cooker in cold oven. Set oven at 450°F (230°C). Bake, stirring once or twice, until beef is tender, about 2 hours. Remove pickling spices. Garnish with parsley.

Barbecued Pot Roast

2	medium onions, thinly sliced
1	blade-cut or 7-bone chuck roast (3¹/2 to 4 pounds or 1600 to 1800 g), fat trimmed
1	can (6 ounces or 170 g) tomato paste
1	clove garlic, minced
2	tablespoons (30 mL) Worcestershire sauce
2	tablespoons (30 mL) cider vinegar
¹/4	cup (60 mL) packed brown sugar
¹/4	cup (60 mL) sweet pickle relish
¹/4	cup (60 mL) dry red wine
1	teaspoon (5 mL) salt
1	teaspoon (5 mL) dry mustard
	Minced fresh parsley

Favorite barbecue sauce ingredients flavor this tender pot roast, certain to be a hit with the family accompanied by a crisp green cabbage slaw and broad egg noodles.

1. Soak top and bottom of 3¹/4-quart (3.25 L) clay cooker in water about 15 minutes; drain.

2. Spread half the onions over bottom of cooker. Place roast over onions. Cover with remaining onions. Mix remaining ingredients except parsley; pour into cooker.

3. Place covered cooker in cold oven. Set oven at 425°F (220°C). Bake until meat is very tender, 2 to 2¹/2 hours.

4. Carve roast. Skim and discard fat from cooking liquid; spoon liquid over meat. Garnish with parsley.

Italian Meat Loaf

4   mild Italian pork sausages
         (about ³/₄ pound or 340 g)
1   egg
1   can (8 ounces or 225 g) tomato
         sauce
1   cup (250 mL) fresh bread
         crumbs
¹/₂   cup (125 mL) grated Parmesan
         cheese
1   clove garlic, minced
¹/₂   teaspoon (2 mL) salt
¹/₂   teaspoon (2 mL) dried basil
         leaves
1   pound (450 g) ground lean beef

Italian sausages create a zesty mosaic in the center of this colorful meat loaf. Serve it for an easy family meal with a favorite salad, bread sticks or garlic bread and a cooked green vegetable such as zucchini or broccoli.

1. Soak top and bottom of loaf-shaped, 5¹/₂-cup (1375 mL) clay cooker in water about 15 minutes; drain.

2. Pierce each Italian sausage in several places with a fork; arrange in cooker.

3. Place covered cooker in cold oven. Set oven at 450°F (230°C). Bake until sausages begin to brown, about 30 minutes. Pour off and discard drippings.

4. Beat egg in medium bowl. Stir in all but ¹/₄ cup (60 mL) of the tomato sauce, the bread crumbs, cheese, garlic, salt and basil. Add ground beef and mix.

5. Remove sausage from cooker. Taking care not to touch hot cooker, spread half the meat mixture in cooker. Arrange sausages over meat mixture; cover with remaining ground meat mixture. Spread remaining tomato sauce over top.

6. Bake covered until meat loaf is brown, about 1 hour. Let stand covered 3 to 5 minutes before slicing.

Finger-Licking Short Ribs

1   can (8 ounces or 225 g) tomato
         sauce
2   tablespoons (30 mL) honey
2   tablespoons (30 mL) cider
         vinegar
1   tablespoon (15 mL)
         Worcestershire sauce
4   to 5 pounds (1800 to 2250 g)
         beef short ribs
         Salt
         Pepper
1   medium onion, finely chopped
1   clove garlic, minced

Short ribs of beef cooked slowly in clay are meaty, tender and flavorful with a honeyed tomato sauce. Bake potatoes in the same oven to accompany the short ribs.

1. Soak top and bottom of 3¹/₄-quart (3.25 L) clay cooker in water about 15 minutes; drain.

2. Mix tomato sauce, honey, vinegar and Worcestershire sauce in small saucepan. Heat until bubbly; remove from heat. Sprinkle ribs on all sides lightly with salt and pepper. Place in cooker. Sprinkle with onion and garlic. Pour in tomato sauce mixture.

3. Place covered cooker in cold oven. Set oven at 375°F (190°C). Bake until meat is very tender, 3 to 3¹/₂ hours. Skim and discard fat. Serve short ribs with sauce.

Beef in Red Wine

2   medium onions, thinly sliced,
    separated into rings
4   medium carrots, pared, cut into
    1/4-inch (0.5 cm) slices
1   cup (250 mL) julienne-cut ham
    strips, 1x1/2 inch
    (2.5x1.5 cm)
3   pounds (1350 g) lean beef
    chuck, cut into 1-inch
    (2.5 cm) cubes
3   cloves garlic, minced
1   teaspoon (5 mL) dried thyme
    leaves
1/2 teaspoon (2 mL) dried
    rosemary leaves, crumbled
1/2 teaspoon (2 mL) dried
    marjoram leaves
1   bay leaf
1   tablespoon (15 mL) salt
1/4 teaspoon (1 mL) freshly ground
    pepper
1/4 cup (60 mL) brandy, if desired
1 1/2 cups (375 mL) dry red wine
1   can (1 pound or 450 g)
    tomatoes, coarsely chopped,
    liquid reserved

This savory beef stew, thick with vegetables, creates a wonderful aroma in the kitchen as it simmers in red wine seasoned with a medley of herbs. Accompany it with noodles and your favorite green salad.

1. Combine all ingredients except tomatoes in large bowl. Refrigerate covered 2 to 3 hours.

2. Soak top and bottom of 3 1/4-quart (3.25 L) clay cooker in water about 15 minutes; drain.

3. Transfer beef mixture to cooker. Add tomatoes with liquid.

4. Place covered cooker in cold oven. Set oven at 425°F (220°C). Bake, stirring once or twice, until beef and carrots are tender, 2 1/2 to 3 hours.

Baked Flank Steak, Stroganoff Style

1/2 pound (225 g) mushrooms,
    sliced
2   tablespoons (30 mL) butter or
    margarine
1   flank steak (about 1 1/2 pounds
    or 675 g)
    Salt
    Pepper
    Paprika
2   medium onions, thinly sliced,
    separated into rings

Moistly cooked flank steak, rolled with sautéed mushrooms, is sauced with an abundance of piquant, oniony cream. Accompany it with rice or noodles.

1. Soak top and bottom of 2-quart (2 L) clay cooker in water about 15 minutes; drain.

2. Sauté mushrooms in butter in skillet until light brown. Lightly sprinkle both sides of flank steak with salt, pepper and paprika. Spread about half the cooked mushrooms down center of flank steak. Roll up, beginning at long side.

BAKED FLANK STEAK, STROGANOFF STYLE, continued

1   clove garlic, minced
1/2 cup (125 mL) regular-strength
      beef broth, canned or
      homemade
1/3 cup (80 mL) dry white wine
1   tablespoon (15 mL)
      Worcestershire sauce
2   teaspoons (10 mL) cornstarch
1   tablespoon (15 mL) water
1/2 cup (125 mL) sour cream
      Minced fresh parsley

3. Place flank steak in cooker. Cover with remaining mushrooms, the onion rings and garlic. Mix broth, wine and Worcestershire sauce; pour into cooker.

4. Place covered cooker in cold oven. Set oven at 425°F (220°C). Bake until beef is very tender, 1 1/2 to 2 hours.

5. Remove cooking liquid, mushrooms and onions to skillet. Cover cooker to keep meat warm. Mix cornstarch and water; stir into skillet. Heat and stir until mixture boils; cook, stirring constantly, until thickened. Remove from heat; stir in sour cream. Cook over low heat just until hot (do not boil).

6. Cut flank steak roll into 1/2-inch (1.5 cm) thick slices; pour sour cream sauce over meat. Garnish with parsley.

Makes 6 to 8 servings

Steak and Kidney Pie

1/2 pound (225 g) mushrooms, cut
      into quarters
2   tablespoons (30 mL) butter or
      margarine
1 1/2 pounds (675 g) boneless top
      round, cut into 1/2-inch
      (1.5 cm) cubes
1/2 pound (225 g) beef or lamb
      kidneys, cut into 1/4-inch
      (0.5 cm) slices
1/4 cup (60 mL) all-purpose flour
1 1/2 teaspoons (7 mL) salt
1/4 teaspoon (1 mL) pepper
1/4 teaspoon (1 mL) dried
      marjoram leaves
1/4 teaspoon (1 mL) dried thyme
      leaves
1/2 teaspoon (2 mL) dried summer
      savory leaves
2/3 cup (160 mL) regular-strength
      beef broth, canned or
      homemade
1   package (10 ounces or 285 g)
      frozen patty shells, thawed
1   egg
1   teaspoon (5 mL) water

As if in a little clay oven, the top crust of this traditional English meat pie browns crisply and beautifully. Cooks in a hurry will appreciate how easily the pastry is made; it's formed from thawed, frozen patty shells. The mixture of tender meat is rich and savory, without any precooking.

1. Soak top and bottom of 2- to 3 1/4-quart (2 to 3.25 L) clay cooker in water about 15 minutes; drain.

2. Sauté mushrooms in butter until light brown.

3. Coat beef cubes and kidneys with mixture of flour, salt, pepper and herbs. Place half the meat mixture in cooker; cover with sautéed mushrooms; top with remaining meat mixture. Pour in broth.

4. Arrange patty shells, overlapping slightly, on floured board or pastry cloth. Roll out into shape of cooker. Place pastry over meat mixture, turning edge under and pressing firmly against sides. Cut several slits in pastry to allow steam to escape. Mix egg and 1 teaspoon (5 mL) water; brush over pastry.

5. Place covered cooker in cold oven. Set oven at 425°F (220°C). Bake until meat is tender (insert long skewer to test) and crust is brown, about 2 hours.

Belgian Beef Baked in Beer

3 **pounds (1350 g) boneless beef chuck, fat trimmed, cut into 1-inch (2.5 cm) cubes**
2 **tablespoons (30 mL) flour**
1¹/₂ **teaspoons (7 mL) salt**
¹/₈ **teaspoon (0.5 mL) white pepper**
¹/₂ **teaspoon (2 mL) dried rosemary leaves**
4 **medium onions, thinly sliced, separated into rings**
1 **clove garlic, minced**
1 **small bay leaf**
3 **whole cloves**
1 **can or bottle (12 ounces or 375 mL) beer**
2 **tablespoons (30 mL) red wine vinegar**
1 **teaspoon (5 mL) Dijon-style mustard**
   Minced fresh parsley

Oven stews are particularly easy in a clay cooker, as they require no tedious and messy range-top browning. Just coat pieces of meat with seasonings and a little flour, and place them in a clay cooker with onions, vegetables and liquid. This one is delicious with Braised Belgian Endive (see Index for page number) and fluffy mashed potatoes.

1. Soak top and bottom of 3¹/₄-quart (3.25 L) clay cooker in water about 15 minutes; drain.

2. Coat beef cubes with mixture of flour, salt, pepper and rosemary. Place beef cubes in cooker. Stir in onions, garlic, bay leaf and cloves. Pour in beer.

3. Place covered cooker in cold oven. Set oven at 425°F (220°C). Bake, stirring once or twice, until beef is very tender, 2¹/₂ to 3 hours.

4. Stir vinegar and mustard into meat mixture. Garnish with parsley.

Chili Beef Stew

1 **cup (250 mL) dried red kidney beans**
2 **cups (500 mL) water**
3 **pounds (1350 g) boneless beef chuck, fat trimmed, cut into 1-inch (2.5 cm) cubes**
2 **tablespoons (30 mL) flour**
2 **tablespoons (30 mL) chili powder**
1¹/₂ **teaspoons (7 mL) salt**
1 **teaspoon (5 mL) ground cumin**
1 **medium onion, chopped**
2 **cloves garlic, minced**
1 **can (4 ounces or 115 g) diced green chiles**
1 **can (1 pound or 450 g) tomatoes, coarsely chopped, liquid reserved**
1 **cup (250 mL) shredded Monterey Jack cheese**
1 **avocado, peeled, sliced**

Here is a really hearty chili with red beans and lots of beef. Serve it south-of-the-border style, sprinkling on melty cheese and adding a garland of avocado slices. It is good with warm buttered corn tortillas and cold beer.

1. Heat beans and 2 cups (500 mL) water in medium saucepan to boiling. Boil briskly 2 minutes; remove from heat. Let stand covered 1 hour.

2. Soak top and bottom of 3¹/₄-quart (3.25 L) clay cooker about 15 minutes; drain.

3. Coat beef cubes with mixture of flour, chili powder, salt and cumin. Place beef cubes in cooker. Stir in onion, garlic, green chiles and beans with water. Pour in tomatoes with liquid.

4. Place covered cooker in cold oven. Set oven at 450°F (230°C). Bake stirring once or twice, until beans and beef are tender, about 2 hours.

5. Sprinkle with cheese; garnish with avocado slices.

Beef Shanks Piedmontese

Makes 6 servings

6   beef shanks (3 to 3¹/2 pounds or
      1350 to 1600 g), about
      ³/4-inch (2 cm) thick
      Salt
      Pepper
      Flour
1   medium onion, finely chopped
1   clove garlic, minced
1   large carrot, pared, shredded
1   rib celery, finely chopped
1   small bay leaf
4   whole cloves
¹/4 teaspoon (1 mL) dried
      rosemary leaves
1   cup (250 mL) dry red wine
1   tablespoon (15 mL) tomato
      paste
3   tablespoons (45 mL) rum
¹/2 cup (125 mL) regular-strength
      beef broth, canned or
      homemade
      Minced fresh parsley

From Northern Italy, this vegetable-rich treatment of beef shanks is appealing with a delicate pasta such as homemade tagliarini. Serve with a hearty red wine.

1. Soak top and bottom of 3¹/4-quart (3.25 L) clay cooker in water about 15 minutes; drain.

2. Sprinkle beef shanks on all sides lightly with salt and pepper; coat with flour, tapping to remove excess.

3. Combine vegetables, bay leaf, cloves and rosemary. Mix wine and tomato paste. Place beef shanks in cooker; cover with vegetable mixture; pour in wine mixture.

4. Place covered cooker in cold oven. Set oven at 425°F (220°C). Bake until meat is very tender, about 2¹/2 hours.

5. Remove beef shanks to warm serving bowl; keep warm. Discard bay leaf. Skim and discard fat from vegetable mixture; process in blender or food processor until smooth. Stir rum and broth into purée; heat to boiling. Taste and add salt, if needed. Pour sauce over beef shanks. Garnish with parsley.

Roast Beef with Garlic Potatoes

Makes 8 servings

1   rolled boneless cross-rib or
      sirloin tip beef roast (4¹/4 to
      4¹/2 pounds or 1900 g to
      2 kg)
3   medium baking potatoes,
      pared, cut lengthwise into 6
      wedges
¹/4 cup (60 mL) butter or
      margarine
2   cloves garlic, minced
¹/4 teaspoon (1 mL) dried thyme
      leaves
¹/8 teaspoon (0.5 mL) paprika
¹/8 teaspoon (0.5 mL) seasoned
      pepper

Tender roasts can be cooked as rare as you like them in a clay cooker. Use a meat thermometer to be sure of the doneness you prefer. In this recipe, meat and potatoes are cooked together conveniently in a covered clay pot of medium size. Both are drizzled with seasoned garlic butter.

1. Soak top and bottom of 3¹/4-quart (3.25 L) clay cooker in water about 15 minutes; drain.

2. Place roast, fat side up, in cooker; surround wih potato wedges. Melt butter in small pan; stir in remaining ingredients. Pour butter mixture evenly over meat and potatoes. Insert meat thermometer in thickest part of roast.

3. Place covered cooker in cold oven. Set oven at 425°F (220°C). Bake until meat is about 5°F (3°C) below desired temperature [135°F (57°C) for rare, 145°F (63°C) for medium-rare to medium], 1³/4 hours to 2¹/4 hours. Remove cover; bake until meat and potatoes brown, 5 to 10 minutes.

4. Cut roast into thin slices. Arrange meat and potatoes on warm serving platter; spoon cooking juices over meat and potatoes.

Clay Cooker London "Broil"

1/4 **cup (60 mL) salad oil**
1/4 **cup (60 mL) dry sherry**
2   **cloves garlic, minced**
1   **tablespoon (15 mL) Worcestershire sauce**
1   **teaspoon (5 mL) Dijon-style mustard**
1/2 **teaspoon (2 mL) salt**
1/4 **teaspoon (1 mL) sugar**
1/4 **teaspoon (1 mL) dried summer savory leaves**
2   **to 3 pounds (900 to 1350 g) first-cut top round, about 1 1/2 inches (4 cm) thick**
1   **bay leaf**
     Freshly ground pepper
     Minced fresh parsley

When the thick, relatively tender first-cut of top round is marinated and cooked in a clay pot, the result is similar to that achieved by broiling the beef — yet the meat is both neater to cook and juicier.

1. Place oil, sherry, garlic, Worcestershire sauce, mustard, salt, sugar and summer savory in blender container or jar with tight-fitting lid; process or shake until mixed. Pour over meat in shallow baking dish, turning meat to coat. Insert bay leaf in marinade. Refrigerate covered with plastic wrap at least 8 hours or overnight.

2. Soak top and bottom of 2-quart (2 L) clay cooker in water about 15 minutes; drain.

3. Remove meat from marinade and place in cooker. Grind pepper generously over top of meat. Insert meat thermometer in thickest part of meat.

4. Place covered cooker in cold oven. Set oven at 475°F (250°C). Bake until thermometer registers 130°F (55°C), 40 to 45 minutes. Remove cooking liquid with baster. Bake meat uncovered until brown, about 5 minutes.

5. Cut meat into thin diagonal slices. Garnish with parsley.

Crusty Rack of Lamb

1   **rack of lamb (1 3/4 to 2 pounds or 800 to 900 g), 6 to 8 ribs**
     Salt
     White pepper
1   **tablespoon (15 mL) Dijon-style mustard**
2   **teaspoons (10 mL) olive or salad oil**
1   **clove garlic, minced**
1   **teaspoon (5 mL) dry vermouth**
1   **tablespoon (15 mL) minced fresh parsley**
1/2 **teaspoon (2 mL) dried oregano leaves**
1/4 **teaspoon (1 mL) dried thyme leaves**
1/2 **cup (125 mL) fresh bread crumbs**

A zippy mustard and garlic-flavored bread crumb mixture coats a rack of lamb for two. For this very French treatment, cook the lamb in the French style — rare in the center.

1. Soak top and bottom of 2-quart (2 L) clay cooker in water about 15 minutes; drain.

2. Trim and discard surface fat from lamb; sprinkle lamb on all sides with salt and pepper. Place lamb, rounded side up, in cooker. Insert meat thermometer in center of thickest part of meat.

3. Place covered cooker in cold oven. Set oven at 475°F (250°C). Bake 35 minutes. While lamb is baking, combine mustard, oil, garlic, vermouth, parsley and herbs; stir in bread crumbs.

4. Press bread crumb mixture over top of lamb. Bake uncovered until bread crumbs brown and thermometer registers 145°F (63°C), 10 to 15 minutes. Carve between ribs to serve.

Happy Anniversary
Love
Judith

Dilled Leg of Lamb with Lemon Sauce

1   leg of lamb (4¹/2 to 5 pounds or 2 kg to 2250 g)
3   cloves garlic, cut into slivers
1   lemon
1   teaspoon (5 mL) dried dill weed
¹/8   teaspoon (0.5 mL) white pepper
¹/4   cup (60 mL) dry white wine
1   medium onion, thinly sliced
    Regular-strength chicken broth, canned or homemade, if needed
1   teaspoon (5 mL) cornstarch
1   tablespoon (15 mL) water
1   egg yolk
¹/2   teaspoon (2 mL) salt

The light and lively sauce for this deeply flavorful leg of lamb is also good over steamed broccoli or asparagus spears and new potatoes cooked in their jackets.

1. Soak top and bottom of 3¹/4- to 4³/4-quart (3.25 to 4.75 L) clay cooker in water about 15 minutes; drain.

2. Cut slits in fat covering lamb; insert garlic slivers. Place leg of lamb in cooker. Insert meat thermometer in thickest part of meat. Grate lemon rind; squeeze juice. Mix lemon rind, dill weed and pepper; sprinkle over lamb. Pour in lemon juice and wine. Arrange onion slices around lamb.

3. Place covered cooker in cold oven. Set oven at 425°F (220°C). Bake 1¹/4 to 2 hours, until meat thermometer registers 5°F (3°C) below desired temperature — 140° to 145°F (about 60°C) for rare, 160°F (70°C) for medium, or 170°F (75°C) for well-done.

4. Pour off and reserve cooking liquid and onions. Cover cooker to keep meat warm. Skim and discard fat from cooking liquid. Measure cooking liquid with onions; if necessary, add broth to make 1¹/2 cups (375 mL).

5. Pour liquid and onions into skillet. Mix cornstarch and 1 tablespoon (15 mL) water; stir into skillet. Heat to boiling; cook, stirring constantly, until thickened and clear. Beat egg in small bowl; gradually beat in a little of the sauce. Stir egg mixture into sauce; cook over medium heat, stirring constantly, just until thickened (do not boil). Stir in salt.

6. Carve lamb; spoon sauce over each serving.

Cassoulet

1   cup (250 mL) dried small white beans, rinsed
4   cups (1 L) cold water
2   pounds (900 g) boneless lamb shoulder, fat trimmed, cut into 1-inch (2.5 cm) cubes
1   large onion, chopped
1   medium carrot, pared, shredded
2   cloves garlic, minced
¹/2   teaspoon (2 mL) dried thyme leaves

This classic French casserole mixes white beans, smoked ham, lamb and sausage. Neither too dry nor too solid with beans in this interpretation, it is handsomely crusted with crisp bread crumbs. It makes a good buffet dish with French bread and a green salad.

1. Place beans in 4 cups (1 L) water in deep bowl; let stand 8 hours or overnight. [Or, heat beans and 4 cups (1 L) water in 2-quart (2 L) saucepan, to boiling, boil briskly 2 minutes. Remove from heat. Let stand covered 1 hour.]

2. Soak top and bottom of 3¹/4-quart (3.25 L) clay cooker in water about 15 minutes; drain.

CASSOULET, continued

1   can (8 ounces or 225 g) tomato
        sauce
1   bay leaf
1   large smoked ham hock (about
        1 pound or 450 g)
1   pound (450 g) Polish or
        smoked sausage
2   tablespoons (30 mL) butter or
        margarine
1   tablespoon (15 mL) salad oil
1 1/2 cups (375 mL) fresh French
        bread crumbs

3. Combine beans with liquid, lamb, onion, carrot, garlic and thyme in clay cooker. Stir in tomato sauce. Insert bay leaf and ham hock in center.

4. Place covered cooker in cold oven. Set oven at 375°F (190°C). Bake, stirring once or twice, until ham, lamb and beans are tender, about 3 hours.

5. Cut sausage into 1 1/2-inch (4 cm) pieces; pierce each piece with fork. Heat butter and oil in frying pan; stir bread crumbs in oil mixture until well coated.

6. Remove ham hock from cooker. When cool enough to handle, discard bones and skin; cut meat into chunks. Return meat to cooker. Stir in sausage. Sprinkle evenly with bread crumbs.

7. Bake uncovered until sausage is hot and bread crumbs are crisp and brown, about 35 minutes.

Makes 8 to 10 servings

Lamb Shoulder Roast with Rice Pilaf Stuffing

1   tablespoon (15 mL) salad oil
1   tablespoon (15 mL) butter or
        margarine
1/2 cup (125 mL) uncooked long-
        grain white rice
1/4 cup (60 mL) finely chopped
        onion
2   tablespoons (30 mL) slivered
        almonds
1   large can (15 ounces or 425 g)
        tomato sauce
1/3 cup (80 mL) regular-strength
        chicken broth, canned or
        homemade
1   clove garlic, minced
2   tablespoons (30 mL) dark
        raisins
1/2 teaspoon (2 mL) cinnamon
1/4 teaspoon (1 mL) ground
        coriander
1/4 teaspoon (1 mL) dried mint
        leaves
1   boneless lamb shoulder roast
        (4 1/2 to 5 pounds or 2 kg to
        2250 g), fat trimmed
1/2 cup (125 mL) dry white wine

Armenian cooking influences this boned lamb roast, with a stuffing of spiced rice, raisins and almonds. Accompany it with crisp flat bread, a cucumber salad and a fruity California Gamay Beaujolais.

1. Heat oil and butter in medium skillet; add rice, onion and almonds. Cook, stirring frequently, just until beginning to brown. Stir in 1/2 cup (125 mL) of the tomato sauce, the broth, garlic, raisins, cinnamon, coriander and mint. Heat to boiling; reduce heat. Simmer covered 10 minutes (rice will be chewy).

2. Soak top and bottom of 3 1/4-quart (3.25 L) clay cooker in water about 15 minutes; drain.

3. Fill cavity in lamb roast with rice mixture; sew edges closed with clean white string or heavy thread. Place roast, fat side up, in cooker. Insert meat thermometer in thickest part of meat. Mix remaining tomato sauce and the wine; pour into cooker.

4. Place covered cooker in cold oven. Set oven at 425°F (220°C). Bake until lamb is tender and brown and thermometer registers 160°F (70°C), 1 1/2 to 1 3/4 hours.

5. Remove strings or thread from roast; cut into 1/2-inch (1.5 cm) slices. Skim and discard fat from cooking liquid; spoon over lamb.

Makes 8 servings

Moussaka in an Eggplant Robe

2 medium eggplants, each about
    1¼ pounds (550 g), unpared
  Salt
¼ cup (60 mL) olive or salad oil
    (approximately)
2 eggs
1 cup (250 mL) fresh bread
    crumbs
1 large onion, finely chopped
2 cloves garlic, minced
2 teaspoons (10 mL) paprika
1 teaspoon (5 mL) salt
½ teaspoon (2 mL) dried
    rosemary leaves, crumbled
2 pounds (900 g) ground lamb
  Tomato Sauce with Mushrooms
    (recipe follows)
  Parsley sprigs

Moussaka, the hearty Greek lamb and eggplant casserole, takes many forms. Baked in a clay cooker lined with the eggplant skins, then turned out in a perfect loaf, it makes an attractive presentation.

1. Cut stems from eggplants; cut lengthwise into quarters. Sprinkle cut surfaces with salt; let stand 20 minutes. Pat dry with paper toweling.

2. Soak top and bottom of 3¼-quart (3.25 L) clay cooker in water about 15 minutes; drain.

3. Place eggplant wedges on rack in broiler pan. Brush generously with oil. Broil about 6 inches (15 cm) from heat, brushing with additional oil if needed, until brown, about 15 minutes. Scoop eggplant from skins, leaving skins intact. Brush eggplant skins on both sides with remaining oil. Line bottom and sides of cooker with skins, dark sides toward center. Cut eggplant into ½-inch (1.5 cm) cubes.

4. Beat eggs lightly; stir in bread crumbs, onion, garlic, paprika, 1 teaspoon (5 mL) salt and the rosemary. Add lamb and eggplant. Spread mixture in cooker.

5. Place covered cooker in cold oven. Set oven at 425°F (220°C). Bake until lamb is firm in center and top is brown, about 1¾ hours. Spoon off and discard fat. Let stand covered 5 minutes.

6. While Moussaka is baking, make Tomato Sauce with Mushrooms. Loosen edges of Moussaka with spatula. Invert onto warm serving platter. Spoon some tomato sauce down the center. Garnish with parsley. Cut into thick slices and serve with remaining Tomato Sauce.

Makes about 2 cups (500 mL)

Tomato Sauce with Mushrooms

1 large onion, finely chopped
3 tablespoons (45 mL) butter or
    margarine
¼ pound (115 g) mushrooms,
    sliced
1 can (16 ounces or 450 g)
    tomatoes, coarsely chopped,
    liquid reserved
½ cup (125 mL) regular-strength
    chicken broth, canned or
    homemade
½ teaspoon (2 mL) salt
¼ teaspoon (1 mL) white pepper
¼ teaspoon (1 mL) dried oregano
    leaves
¼ teaspoon (1 mL) sugar

1. Sauté onion in butter in 2-quart (2 L) saucepan until soft. Stir in mushrooms; sauté until light brown. Stir in remaining ingredients. Heat to boiling; reduce heat. Simmer covered 15 minutes.

2. Remove cover; cook over medium-high heat, stirring occasionally, until thick, about 30 minutes.

Irish Stew

2	pounds (900 g) boneless lamb shoulder, fat trimmed, cut into 1-inch (2.5 cm) cubes
1	tablespoon (15 mL) flour
1	teaspoon (5 mL) salt
1/2	teaspoon (2 mL) paprika
1/8	teaspoon (0.5 mL) white pepper
1	medium onion, thinly sliced, separated into rings
2	ribs celery, thinly sliced
2	cloves garlic, minced
1/4	teaspoon (1 mL) whole cloves
3	medium carrots, pared, cut into 1/2-inch (1.5 cm) slices
3	medium new potatoes, pared, cut into 1/4-inch (0.5 cm) slices
1	bay leaf
1	cup (250 mL) regular-strength beef broth, canned or homemade
1	cup (250 mL) frozen peas, thawed

Here is another oven stew that is a breeze to prepare — just layer seasoned, floured cubes of lamb with vegetables, pour in broth and bake. Add the peas just at the end to keep their brilliant color accent.

1. Soak top and bottom of 3 1/4-quart (3.25 L) clay cooker in water about 15 minutes; drain.

2. Coat lamb cubes with mixture of flour, salt, paprika and pepper. Combine onion, celery, garlic and cloves. Place a third of the lamb in cooker; top with carrots and half the onion mixture. Add a third of the lamb, the remaining onion mixture and the potatoes. Top with remaining lamb. Insert bay leaf. Pour in broth.

3. Place covered cooker in cold oven. Set oven at 425°F (220°C). Bake, stirring gently once or twice, until lamb and vegetables are tender and top browns, about 2 hours. Turn off oven. Stir in peas. Cover cooker and return to oven until peas are hot, 5 to 10 minutes.

Potato-Topped Lamb Casserole

6	thick lamb shoulder or hip blocks (about 3 1/4 pounds or 1450 g), fat trimmed
	Salt
	White pepper
2	medium onions, finely chopped
1	clove garlic, minced
1/4	cup (60 mL) minced fresh parsley
4	whole cloves
3	medium baking potatoes, pared, thinly sliced
2	tablespoons (30 mL) butter or margarine

Sliced potatoes bake in a golden layer over thick lamb chops called lamb blocks, cut from either shoulder or hip. This meat and potato casserole can go directly from oven to table for serving.

1. Soak top and bottom of 3 1/4-quart (3.25 L) clay cooker in water about 15 minutes; drain.

2. Sprinkle lamb chops on both sides with salt and pepper. Place lamb in cooker. Add onions, garlic, parsley and cloves. Cover with even layer of potatoes; sprinkle with salt and pepper. Dot with butter.

3. Place covered cooker in cold oven. Set oven at 450°F (230°C). Bake until lamb and potatoes are tender, about 1 hour. Remove cover; bake until potatoes are brown, 20 to 25 minutes.

Makes 4 servings

Lamb Shanks in Chablis

4 lamb shanks (about 1 pound or 450 g)
3 cloves garlic, cut into slivers
   Salt
   Coarsely ground pepper
4 small new potatoes, scrubbed
4 small carrots, pared
1 medium onion, finely chopped
1 cup (250 mL) dry Chablis
   Minced fresh parsley

Simple seasonings and vegetables combine with moistly tender lamb shanks to produce a sensational tasting combination, thanks to cooking in clay. With meat and vegetables all in one dish, you need only a salad to complete this meal.

1. Soak top and bottom of 3 1/4-quart (3.25 L) clay cooker in water about 15 minutes; drain.

2. Cut slits in lamb shanks; insert garlic slivers. Place lamb shanks in cooker. Sprinkle with salt and pepper. Pare 1-inch (2.5 cm) strip around center of each potato. Add potatoes and carrots to cooker. Sprinkle with onion. Pour in wine.

3. Place covered cooker in cold oven. Set oven at 425°F (220°C). Bake until lamb shanks are brown and very tender, about 2 hours. Remove lamb shanks and vegetables to warm serving platter; keep warm. Skim and discard fat from cooking liquid. Spoon cooking liquid over meat and vegetables; garnish with parsley.

Makes 6 servings

Swiss Veal Strips

1 3/4 to 2 pounds (800 to 900 g) thinly sliced boneless veal
2 tablespoons (30 mL) flour
1 teaspoon (5 mL) salt
1/2 teaspoon (2 mL) paprika
1/8 teaspoon (0.5 mL) ground nutmeg
   Pinch white pepper
1 small onion, finely chopped
1/2 pound (225 g) mushrooms, cut into quarters
3/4 cup (180 mL) dry white wine
1/2 cup (125 mL) whipping cream
3 tablespoons (45 mL) brandy
   Chopped fresh parsley

Flamed with brandy, this veal dish can make a dramatic party entrée. Serve with a dry white wine and fine homemade noodles or buttery hash-browned potatoes.

1. Soak top and bottom of 2-quart (2 L) clay cooker in water about 15 minutes; drain.

2. Cut veal into strips 2x3/4 inch (5x2 cm). Coat veal with mixture of flour, salt, paprika, nutmeg and pepper.

3. Place veal, onion, mushrooms and wine in cooker.

4. Place covered cooker in cold oven. Set oven at 425°F (220°C). Bake, stirring once or twice, until veal is tender and light brown, 1 1/2 to 2 hours.

5. Pour cooking liquid into skillet. Cover cooker to keep veal warm. Add cream to cooking liquid. Heat to boiling, cook, stirring constantly, until slightly thickened. Pour sauce over veal.

6. Warm brandy in small saucepan. Ignite and pour flaming over veal. Stir sauce into veal until flames die. Garnish with parsley.

Makes 9 servings

Roast Veal Orloff

1 boneless veal shoulder roast
(3 pounds or 1350 g), rolled,
tied
3 tablespoons (45 mL) butter or
margarine
Onion-Cheese Sauce (recipe
follows)
8 thin slices prosciutto,
Westphalian ham or other
smoked ham
8 thin slices aged Swiss cheese
1/2 cup (125 mL) fresh bread
crumbs

Here is a spectacular main dish of Belgian and French origin. Prepare this princely dish by first roasting the veal, then slicing the meat almost to the bottom. Fill the spaces between with ham, cheese and a thick, Onion-Cheese Sauce. After the roast is reassembled, it goes back into the oven until it is hot and golden-glazed. Accompany it with noodles and whole green beans.

1. Soak top and bottom of 2-quart (2 L) clay cooker in water about 15 minutes; drain.

2. Place roast, fat side up, in cooker. Dot with 1 tablespoon (15 mL) of the butter. Insert meat thermometer in thickest part of roast.

3. Place covered cooker in cold oven. Set oven at 425°F (220°C). Bake until thermometer registers 165°F (75°C), about 1 3/4 hours.

4. Make Onion-Cheese Sauce.

5. Remove roast from cooker, and remove strings from roast. Being careful to keep shape, cut roast into 9 equal slices, cutting almost to bottom of each slice. Spread cut surfaces with Onion-Cheese Sauce. Insert 1 ham slice and 1 cheese slice in each space. Secure roast with long skewers. Place in cooker.

6. Spread remaining sauce over top of roast. Melt remaining 2 tablespoons (30 mL) butter; stir in bread crumbs. Sprinkle bread crumbs over sauce. Bake roast, uncovered, until crumbs are brown and crisp, 20 to 30 minutes.

7. Place roast on warm serving platter. Stir cooking liquid to form a smooth sauce. To serve, remove skewers from roast and complete slicing. Accompany with sauce.

Makes about 2 cups (500 mL)

Onion-Cheese Sauce

1 medium onion, finely chopped
1/3 cup (80 mL) butter or
margarine
1/4 cup (60 mL) flour
1/4 teaspoon (1 mL) salt
1/8 teaspoon (0.5 mL) ground
nutmeg
Pinch white pepper
1 cup (250 mL) milk
1/3 cup (80 mL) regular-strength
chicken broth, canned or
homemade
1/4 cup (60 mL) shredded Swiss
cheese
2 tablespoons (30 mL) grated
Parmesan cheese

1. Sauté onion in butter in medium saucepan until soft but not brown. Stir in flour, salt, nutmeg and pepper; cook, stirring constantly, until bubbly. Remove from heat.

2. Stir milk and chicken broth into saucepan gradually. Cook over medium heat, stirring constantly, until thick; reduce heat to low. Cook, stirring constantly, 2 minutes. Add cheeses; stir until melted.

40

Creamy French Veal Stew

2 pounds (900 g) boneless veal
shoulder, cut into 1-inch
(2.5 cm) cubes
1/2 pound (225 g) mushrooms, cut
into quarters
1 small onion, finely chopped
1 teaspoon (5 mL) salt
1/4 teaspoon (1 mL) dried tarragon
leaves
1/8 teaspoon (0.5 mL) ground
nutmeg
1/8 teaspoon (0.5 mL) white
pepper
1 tablespoon (15 mL) lemon
juice
2 teaspoons (10 mL) Dijon-style
mustard
1/2 cup (125 mL) dry white wine
1/2 cup (125 mL) whipping cream

Known in France as blanquette de veau, *this dish is said to be a standard in every French housewife's repertoire. It is never easier to make than when you put it together in a clay cooker. This stew is good with rice.*

1. Soak top and bottom of 2-quart (2 L) clay cooker in water about 15 minutes; drain.

2. Place half the veal in cooker. Cover with mushrooms and onion. Top with remaining veal. Sprinkle with salt, tarragon, nutmeg and pepper. Stir lemon juice gradually into mustard in small bowl until smooth; stir in wine. Pour wine mixture over veal and vegetables.

3. Place covered cooker in cold oven. Set oven at 425°F (220°C). Bake, stirring once or twice, until veal and onion are tender, about 1 1/2 hours.

4. Pour cooking liquid into large skillet. Cover cooker to keep veal warm. Add cream to cooking liquid. Heat to boiling; boil stirring occasionally, until reduced by about a third and slightly thickened. Pour sauce over veal.

Veal Marengo

3 pounds (1350 g) boneless veal
shoulder, cut into 1-inch
(2.5 cm) cubes
2 tablespoons (30 mL) flour
1 1/2 teaspoons (7 mL) salt
1/8 teaspoon (0.5 mL) seasoned
pepper
1 teaspoon (5 mL) dried thyme
leaves
1 large onion, finely chopped
1 clove garlic, minced
1/2 cup (125 mL) pimiento-stuffed
olives, rinsed
1/2 pound (225 g) mushrooms, cut
into quarters
1 bay leaf
1 can (1 pound or 450 g)
tomatoes, coarsely chopped,
liquid reserved
1/2 cup (125 mL) dry white wine
Minced fresh parsley

Pimiento-stuffed green olives, mushrooms and tomatoes give veal a more pronounced character in this French stew.

1. Soak top and bottom of 3 1/4-quart (3.25 L) clay cooker in water about 15 minutes; drain.

2. Coat veal with mixture of flour, salt, pepper and thyme. Place veal in cooker. Top with onion, garlic, olives, mushrooms and bay leaf. Pour in tomatoes with liquid and wine.

3. Place covered cooker in cold oven. Set oven at 425°F (220°C). Bake, stirring once or twice, until veal is tender and brown, about 2 1/2 hours. Remove bay leaf. Garnish with parsley.

Veal Breast Stuffed with Spinach, Veal and Ham

Makes 6 servings

1/2   **pound (225 g) ground ham**
1/2   **pound (225 g) ground veal**
1/2   **pound (225 g) mushrooms, finely chopped**
1   **medium onion, finely chopped**
1   **clove garlic, minced**
1   **teaspoon (5 mL) dried tarragon leaves**
1   **package (10 ounces or 285 g) frozen chopped spinach, thawed**
1   **cup (250 mL) shredded Swiss cheese**
1   **cup (250 mL) fresh bread crumbs**
1   **egg, slightly beaten**
1 1/2 **teaspoons (7 mL) salt**
1/8   **teaspoon (0.5 mL) ground nutmeg**
1/8   **teaspoon (0.5 mL) white pepper**
1   **veal breast (3 to 3 1/2 pounds or 1350 to 1600 g) with pocket cut for stuffing**
1/2   **cup (125 mL) regular-strength chicken broth, canned or homemade**
1/2   **cup (125 mL) dry white wine**

There is so little meat on a veal breast that at first glance it might seem scarcely worth cooking. Resourceful Northern Italian cooks, however, know better. They stuff a pocket in this lean, distinctive cut of veal with a spinach, cheese, mushroom and ground meat filling — making a dish fit for a feast. Have your meat dealer cut the pocket along the rib bones at the time you buy the meat.

1. Soak top and bottom of 3 1/4-quart (3.25 L) clay cooker in water about 15 minutes; drain.

2. Combine ground ham, ground veal, the mushrooms, onion, garlic and tarragon. Squeeze spinach to remove liquid. Stir spinach, cheese, bread crumbs, egg, salt, nutmeg and pepper into meat mixture.

3. Pack stuffing lightly into pocket of veal breast; close opening with thread or skewers. Place meat, rounded side up, in cooker. Pour in broth and wine.

4. Place covered cooker in cold oven. Set oven at 425°F (220°C). Bake until veal is tender and brown, about 2 1/2 hours.

5. Remove string or skewers. Carve between bones to serve.

Italian Veal Birds

Makes 4 to 6 servings

1/2   **cup (125 mL) ground ham**
1/2   **cup (125 mL) ricotta cheese**
1/4   **cup (60 mL) grated Parmesan cheese**
1   **clove garlic, minced**
2   **mushrooms, finely chopped**
1   **tablespoon (15 mL) minced fresh parsley**
1/8   **teaspoon (0.5 mL) ground nutmeg**

Here is another distinctive Italian way of preparing veal. The little veal rolls, stuffed with a ham and cheese filling, are baked in wine that becomes a glistening amber sauce.

1. Soak top and bottom of 2-quart (2 L) clay cooker in water about 15 minutes; drain.

2. Combine ham, ricotta and Parmesan cheeses, garlic, mushrooms, 1 tablespoon (15 mL) parsley and the nutmeg; divide into 12 parts.
(Continued on page 44)

ITALIAN VEAL BIRDS, continued

12 thin slices boneless veal round
        (about 1³/₄ pounds or 800 g)
    Salt
1   tablespoon (15 mL) butter or
        margarine
¹/₄ cup (60 mL) dry white wine
¹/₄ cup (60 mL) Marsala wine
    Minced fresh parsley

3. Place veal slices between pieces of waxed paper; pound each slice with flat side of meat mallet until almost doubled in size. Spread filling down center of each veal slice. Roll up slices, securing with wooden picks, small skewers or string. Sprinkle lightly with salt.

4. Place veal rolls in cooker; dot with butter. Pour in white wine and Marsala.

5. Place covered cooker in cold oven. Set oven at 450°F (230°C). Bake until veal is tender and brown, about 1 ¹/₂ hours. (To ensure the veal browns evenly, carefully turn and rearrange the rolls after about 1 hour of baking.)

6. Pour cooking liquid into small saucepan; cover cooker to keep veal warm. Heat cooking liquid, stirring occasionally, to boiling; cook until slightly thickened. Pour over veal. Garnish with parsley.

Makes 6 servings

Italian Veal Shanks

6   pounds (2700 g) veal shanks,
        cut into 2-inch (5 cm)
        lengths
    Salt
    White pepper
    Ground nutmeg
    Flour
1   medium carrot, pared,
        shredded
1   large onion, finely chopped
4   cloves garlic, minced
1   can (1 pound or 450 g)
        tomatoes, coarsely chopped,
        liquid reserved
¹/₂ cup (125 mL) dry white wine
1   tablespoon (15 mL) salt
1   teaspoon (5 mL) sugar
¹/₂ teaspoon (2 mL) dried thyme
        leaves
¹/₄ teaspoon (1 mL) dried sage
        leaves
¹/₃ cup (80 mL) minced fresh
        parsley
1   tablespoon (15 mL) grated
        lemon rind

The richness of the sauce in which these veal shanks (called osso buco*) cook, comes from slow cooking in clay and from the rich marrow in the bones. An accent of parsley, lemon and garlic — known as* gremolata — *lends a very special final touch. Accompany the veal shanks with the Saffron Rice Pilaf (see Index for page number), baked in a smaller clay cooker.*

1. Soak top and bottom of 4³/₄-quart (4.75 L) clay cooker in water about 15 minutes; drain.

2. Sprinkle veal shanks with salt, pepper and nutmeg; coat lightly with flour. Place veal, carrot, onion and 2 cloves of the garlic in cooker. Combine tomatoes with liquid, wine, 1 tablespoon salt (15 mL), the sugar, thyme and sage; pour into cooker.

3. Place covered cooker in cold oven. Set oven at 425°F (220°C). Bake, stirring once or twice, until veal is very tender, about 2¹/₂ hours.

4. Combine remaining 2 cloves garlic, the parsley and lemon rind. Remove veal shanks to a warm serving bowl. Pour cooking liquid into large skillet. Heat to boiling. Cook, stirring constantly, until thick. Stir in half the parsley mixture. Pour sauce over veal shanks; sprinkle with remaining parsley mixture.

Veal-Stuffed Manicotti

12	manicotti (6 ounces or 170 g)
	Veal Filling (recipe follows)
1	large can (28 ounces or 800 g) tomatoes, coarsely chopped, liquid reserved
1	large onion, chopped
1	medium red bell pepper, chopped
1	cup (250 mL) dry white wine
1	tablespoon (15 mL) dried basil leaves
1	teaspoon (5 mL) sugar
1	teaspoon (5 mL) salt
1/2	cup (125 mL) freshly grated Parmesan cheese

If you have ever prepared manicotti using the standard method, you will appreciate the ease of this clay cooker simplification. The pasta shells are stuffed uncooked, and can be prepared ahead and refrigerated. They cook perfectly in a clay cooker in a wine-accented tomato sauce.

1. Soak top and bottom of 3 1/4-quart (3.25 L) clay cooker in water about 15 minutes; drain.

2. Fill uncooked manicotti with Veal Filling. Combine tomatoes with liquid, onion, red pepper, wine, basil, sugar and salt. Spoon a third of the tomato mixture into cooker. Arrange stuffed manicotti over tomato mixture. Pour in remaining tomato mixture.

3. Place covered cooker in cold oven. Set oven at 425°F (220°C). Bake until manicotti are tender and sauce is thick, 1 1/2 to 1 3/4 hours. Sprinkle with Parmesan cheese. Remove cover; bake until cheese browns, 5 to 10 minutes.

Veal Filling

1	pound (450 g) ground veal
1	cup (250 mL) ricotta cheese
1	cup (250 mL) shredded Monterey Jack cheese
1/4	cup (60 mL) freshly grated Parmesan cheese
1/4	cup (60 mL) minced fresh parsley
1/4	cup (60 mL) finely chopped onion
2	cloves garlic, minced
1	tablespoon (15 mL) dried basil leaves
1/4	teaspoon (1 mL) dried oregano leaves
1/4	teaspoon (1 mL) dried marjoram leaves

1. Combine all ingredients.

Pork Goulash with Sauerkraut

2	pounds (900 g) lean boneless pork, cut into 1-inch (2.5 cm) cubes
1	tablespoon (15 mL) flour
1	tablespoon (15 mL) sweet Hungarian paprika

For a simple sauerkraut dish, try this Eastern European pork goulash with sour cream. Accompany it with Spaetzle *or noodles.*

1. Soak top and bottom of 2-quart (2 L) clay cooker in water about 15 minutes; drain.

PORK GOULASH WITH SAUERKRAUT, continued

1	**teaspoon (5 mL) salt**
2	**large onions, finely chopped**
1	**clove garlic, minced**
1	**teaspoon (5 mL) caraway seeds**
1/2	**cup (125 mL) dry white wine**
1	**large can (27 ounces or 800 g) sauerkraut, well drained**
1	**cup (250 mL) sour cream Minced fresh parsley**

2. Coat pork cubes with mixture of flour, paprika and salt. Place pork in cooker. Stir in onions, garlic and caraway seeds. Pour in wine.

3. Place covered cooker in cold oven. Set oven at 425°F (220°C). Bake until pork is tender, about 1 1/4 hours.

4. Stir in sauerkraut; bake covered 30 minutes. Stir in sour cream; bake covered just until hot, about 10 minutes. Garnish with parsley.

Makes 4 to 6 servings

Deep-Dish Ham Quiche

1	**cup (250 mL) ham strips, 2x1/2 x1/4 inches (5x1.5x0.5 cm)**
2	**tablespoons (30 mL) butter or margarine**
	Quiche Crust (recipe follows)
1	**cup (250 mL) shredded aged Swiss cheese**
3	**eggs**
1	**cup (250 mL) half-and-half Nutmeg**

Pastry browns to flaky crispness in a clay cooker, making an irresistible crust for this traditional tasting — if unconventional looking — quiche. As it bakes it puffs to almost the lightness of a soufflé.

1. Soak top and bottom of 2-quart (2 L) clay cooker in water about 15 minutes; drain.

2. Sauté ham strips in butter until light brown.

3. Make Quiche Crust.

4. Roll pastry out to rectangle, a little larger than top of cooker. Ease it into cooker, pressing it about 2 1/2 inches (6.5 cm) up sides. Turn edges under and press firmly against side of cooker with fork.

5. Spread cheese over the crust. Cover cheese with ham strips. Beat eggs with half-and-half until blended. Pour egg mixture over cheese and ham. Sprinkle lightly with nutmeg.

6. Place covered cooker in cold oven. Set oven at 425°F (220°C). Bake until crust is brown and knife inserted in center of custard comes out clean, 45 to 50 minutes. Remove cover; bake until top browns, 3 to 5 minutes. Cut into strips and serve immediately.

Quiche Crust

1 1/4	**cups (310 mL) all-purpose flour**
1/8	**teaspoon (0.5 mL) salt**
1/2	**cup (125 mL) firm butter or margarine**
3	**tablespoons (45 mL) cold water**

1. Mix flour and salt. Cut in butter until mixture forms coarse crumbs. Stir in cold water until dough cleans side of bowl.

2. Shape dough into a ball.

Garlic Marinated Spareribs

4 pounds (1800 g) country-style spareribs
1 cup (250 mL) cider vinegar
3 cups (750 mL) water
2 teaspoons (10 mL) coriander seeds, coarsely crushed
2 teaspoons (10 mL) cumin seeds, coarsely crushed
5 cloves garlic, cut into slivers
1/4 teaspoon (1 mL) cayenne pepper
2 teaspoons (10 mL) salt
1/4 cup (60 mL) dry white wine

Meaty country-style spareribs, marinated in the Portuguese style are especially good with steamed Swiss chard or spinach and new potatoes.

1. Three to four days before cooking spareribs, place spareribs in deep bowl. Combine remaining ingredients except wine; pour over spareribs. Refrigerate covered turning spareribs occasionally, 3 to 4 days.

2. Soak top and bottom of 3 1/4-quart (3.25 L) clay cooker in water about 15 minutes; drain.

3. Remove spareribs from marinade; place fat sides up in cooker. Discard marinade. Pour wine over meat.

4. Place covered cooker in cold oven. Set oven at 425°F (220°C). Bake until spareribs are tender and brown, about 2 hours.

5. Pour off and reserve cooking liquid; cover cooker to keep meat warm. Skim and discard fat from cooking liquid; pour cooking liquid into saucepan. Heat to boiling; boil until reduced and slightly thickened. Carve meat between ribs; spoon sauce over meat.

Roast Pork with Prunes

1 pork loin roast (3 1/2 to 4 pounds or 1600 to 1800 g)
Salt
Ground ginger
White pepper
1 large onion, finely chopped
1 large carrot, pared, finely chopped
1/2 cup (125 mL) port wine
15 to 20 pitted prunes
1/4 cup (60 mL) whipping cream

From the Southwest of France comes this idea for pork roasted with prunes and savory vegetables, served with a port-flavored creamy sauce. Attractive and simple, it makes a good company dinner.

1. Soak top and bottom of 3 1/4-quart (3.25 L) clay cooker in water about 15 minutes; drain.

2. Place roast, fat side up, in cooker. Sprinkle with salt, ginger and pepper. Combine onion and carrot; surround roast with onion mixture. Pour wine over meat and vegetables. Insert meat thermometer in thickest part of roast.

3. Place covered cooker in cold oven. Set oven at 425°F (220°C). Bake 1 hour. Add prunes to cooker. Bake covered until thermometer registers 170°F (77°C), 30 to 45 minutes.

4. Remove roast to warm serving platter; using slotted spoon, place vegetables and prunes around roast; keep warm. Skim and discard fat from cooking liquid; pour cooking liquid into skillet. Stir in cream. Heat to boiling; cook, stirring occasionally, until slightly thickened.

5. Carve roast between bones; spoon sauce over meat, prunes and vegetables.

Pork Chop Dinner for Two

2   **pork loin chops (1 pound or 450 g), about 1 inch (2.5 cm) thick**
    Salt
    Pepper
    Ground ginger
1   **large yam (about 1¼ pounds or 550 g), pared, cut into long wedges**
1   **orange**
1   **piece cinnamon stick, 2 inches (5 cm) long**

Orange flavors both pork chops and wedges of yam to make a no-fuss supper for two; serve with a leafy salad.

1. Soak top and bottom of 2-quart (2 L) clay cooker in water about 15 minutes; drain.

2. Trim excess fat from pork; sprinkle both sides with salt, pepper and ginger. Place pork in cooker. Arrange yam wedges around pork chops. Grate orange rind; squeeze juice from orange; sprinkle rind and juice over pork and yam. Insert cinnamon stick near center.

3. Place covered cooker in cold oven. Set oven at 450°F (230°C). Bake until pork chops and yams are tender, about 1 hour.

4. Baste with cooking liquid. Bake uncovered until brown, about 5 minutes. Spoon cooking liquid into small saucepan. Heat to boiling; cook, stirring occasionally, until slightly reduced and syrupy, about 2 minutes. Spoon sauce over pork chops and yams.

Ham in Madeira

1   **cooked boneless ham (4 to 5 pounds or 1800 to 2250 g)**
4   **medium onions, each cut into 6 wedges**
½   **cup (125 mL) Madeira wine**
1   **teaspoon (5 mL) Dijon-style mustard**
1   **teaspoon (5 mL) dried juniper berries, coarsely crushed**
½   **cup (125 mL) whipping cream**

Juniper berries, favored in European cooking for flavoring wild game, enhance ham cooked with onions, mustard and Madeira. Sauce for the thinly sliced ham is made by skimming the cooking liquid, then reducing it with cream.

1. Soak top and bottom of 3¼-quart (3.25 L) clay cooker in water about 15 minutes; drain.

2. Place ham, fat side up, in cooker. Score fat. Insert meat thermometer in thickest part of meat. Arrange onions around ham. Combine Madeira, mustard and juniper berries; pour into cooker.

3. Place covered cooker in cold oven. Set oven at 425°F (220°C). Bake until ham is brown and thermometer registers 140°F (60°C), about 2 hours. Pour off and reserve cooking liquid. Cover cooker to keep ham and onions warm.

4. Skim and discard fat from cooking liquid; pour cooking liquid into medium skillet. Stir in cream. Heat to boiling; cook, stirring occasionally until sauce is reduced and slightly thickened.

5. Cut ham into thin slices; arrange onions around ham; spoon sauce over ham and onions.

Indonesian Pork Roast

Makes 8 to 10 servings

1   pork loin roast (4 to 5 pounds or 1800 to 2250 g)
1/2   cup (125 mL) chutney
1/4   cup (60 mL) catsup
2   tablespoons (30 mL) salad oil
1   clove garlic
1   tablespoon (15 mL) soy sauce
1/8   teaspoon (0.5 mL) red pepper sauce
1/2   cup (125 mL) finely chopped dry-roasted peanuts

A marinade with chutney, soy sauce and garlic gives a pork loin roast a distinctly piquant flavor. During clay cooker roasting, chopped peanuts add an attractive and crusty coating. Accompany this special roast with a rice pilaf and a sweet-sour salad of oranges, bananas and papayas.

1. Place pork roast in shallow bowl. Process chutney, catsup, oil, garlic, soy sauce, and red pepper sauce in blender until smooth; pour over pork roast. Refrigerate covered 3 hours or overnight.

2. Soak top and bottom of 3 1/4-quart (3.25 L) clay cooker in water about 15 minutes; drain.

3. Place pork roast, fat side up, in cooker. Pour marinade over roast. Pat peanuts evenly over top and sides. Insert meat thermometer in center of roast.

4. Place covered cooker in cold oven. Set oven at 425°F (220°C). Bake until meat thermometer registers 170°F (77°C), 1 3/4 to 2 hours.

5. Carve roast between rib bones; serve with skimmed meat juices.

Pork Chops with Rhubarb Dressing

Makes 4 servings

1 1/2   pounds (675 g) rhubarb, cut into 1/2-inch (1.5 cm) cubes (about 5 cups or 1250 mL)
4   slices firm-textured bread, cut into 1/2-inch (1.5 cm) cubes
2/3   cup (160 mL) packed brown sugar
2   tablespoons (30 mL) flour
1/2   teaspoon (2 mL) ground cinnamon
1/8   teaspoon (0.5 mL) ground ginger
1   tablespoon (15 mL) melted butter or margarine
4   pork loin or shoulder chops (1 1/2 pounds or 675 g), about 3/4 inch (2 cm) thick
1/2   teaspoon (2 mL) salt
    Pinch white pepper
1/4   teaspoon (1 mL) dried rosemary leaves, crumbled
2   tablespoons (30 mL) dry white wine

In this dish, pork chops are sandwiched and baked between layers of a tart-sweet bread dressing with rosy rhubarb. It makes a fresh spring supper served with asparagus or tiny peas.

1. Soak top and bottom of 3 1/4-quart (3.25 L) clay cooker in water about 15 minutes; drain.

2. Combine rhubarb, bread, brown sugar, flour, cinnamon and ginger.

3. Brush bottom and sides of cooker with butter. Spread half the rhubarb mixture in bottom; top with pork chops. Mix salt, pepper and rosemary; sprinkle over pork. Cover with remaining rhubarb mixture. Drizzle with wine.

4. Place covered cooker in cold oven. Set oven at 450°F (230°C). Bake until pork chops are tender, about 1 hour. Remove cover; bake until top is crisp and brown, about 10 minutes.

Makes 8 servings

Roast Pork with Red Cabbage

1	boneless pork loin roast (2¹/₂ to 3 pounds or 1125 to 1350 g), rolled, tied
3/4	teaspoon (4 mL) dried thyme leaves
1/2	teaspoon (2 mL) salt
1/4	teaspoon (1 mL) pepper
1/4	teaspoon (1 mL) ground allspice
3	cloves garlic, minced
1	medium onion, thinly sliced
1	medium carrot, pared, shredded
1	small head red cabbage (about 1¹/₂ pounds or 675 g), shredded
2	medium tart apples, unpared, chopped
1/4	cup (60 mL) white vinegar
1/8	teaspoon (0.5 mL) ground nutmeg
1	cup (250 mL) dry red wine
1	bay leaf
1	teaspoon (5 mL) cornstarch
1	tablespoon (15 mL) water
	Salt

Select a boned, rolled pork loin roast to cook with sweet-sour red cabbage flavored with apples and red wine. The pork is seasoned with a dry marinade — a mixture of herbs, garlic, salt and pepper that is applied several hours before cooking.

1. Press onto all surfaces of the pork roast a mixture of thyme, salt, pepper, allspice and 1 clove of garlic. Refrigerate covered several hours or overnight.

2. Soak top and bottom of 3¹/₄-quart (3.25 L) clay cooker in water about 15 minutes; drain. Line bottom and sides of cooker with parchment paper, if desired.

3. Combine remaining garlic, the onion, carrot, cabbage, apples, vinegar and nutmeg. Place in cooker. Pour wine over vegetables. Insert bay leaf into vegetable mixture.

4. Place covered cooker in cold oven. Set oven at 450°F (230°C). Bake 45 minutes. Place pork roast in center of vegetables, pushing vegetables to sides. Insert a meat thermometer in thickest part of roast. Reduce oven temperature to 425°F (220°C). Bake covered until thermometer registers 165°F (75°C), about 1¹/₄ hours.

5. Remove roast to warm serving platter; using slotted spoon, place vegetables around roast. Keep warm.

6. Skim and discard fat from cooking liquid; pour cooking liquid into skillet. Mix cornstarch and water; stir into skillet. Heat to boiling; cook, stirring constantly, until thickened. Taste and add salt, if needed.

7. Cut pork into thin slices; serve with vegetables and sauce.

Makes 8 to 10 servings

Alsatian Ham Hocks, Sauerkraut and Sausages

3	cans (27 ounces or 800 g each) sauerkraut
2	bay leaves
8	whole cloves
1	teaspoon (5 mL) dried juniper berries
1	teaspoon (5 mL) white or black peppercorns
2	smoked ham hocks (about 2 pounds or 900 g)

This classic combination called Choucroute Garnie, *from the eastern section of France bordering the Rhine, benefits from lengthy cooking in clay to blend the flavors of sauerkraut, smoked pork, wine and such seasonings as juniper berries and cloves. It is a wonderful party dish for a buffet, with a good rye bread and a well chilled white wine such as an Alsatian Sylvaner or Gewurztraminer.*

1. Soak top and bottom of 4³/₄-quart (4.75 L) clay cooker in water about 15 minutes; drain. Line bottom and sides of cooker with parchment paper.

ALSATIAN HAM HOCKS, continued

3   large onions, thinly sliced
1¹/2   cups (375 mL) dry white wine
8   to 10 small boiling potatoes,
        pared
1   pound (450 g) Polish sausage,
        smoked bratwurst or
        knackwurst
1   pound (450 g) bockwurst
1   pound (450 g) veal frankfurters
        Minced fresh parsley
        Dijon-style mustard

2. Rinse sauerkraut in colander with cold water; drain thoroughly. Combine bay leaves, cloves, juniper berries and peppercorns.

3. Place a third of the sauerkraut in cooker. Add ham hocks. Top with half the onions and half the seasoning mixture. Add a third of the sauerkraut and the remaining onions and seasonings. Cover with remaining sauerkraut. Pour in wine.

4. Place covered cooker in cold oven. Set oven at 425°F (220°C). Bake, stirring once or twice, 2¹/2 hours.

5. Arrange potatoes around edges of cooker. Bake covered 25 minutes.

6. Pierce each sausage in several places with fork; nestle sausages in sauerkraut. Bake covered until sausages are hot and potatoes are tender, 20 to 25 minutes.

7. Mound sauerkraut on warm serving platter; top with skinned ham hocks. Arrange sausage along the sides and potatoes at ends of platter. Sprinkle potatoes with parsley. Serve with mustard.

Makes 8 to 10 servings

Country-Style Spareribs Polynesian

4   to 5 pounds (1800 to 2250 g)
        country-style spareribs, cut
        into serving pieces
1/2   cup (125 mL) soy sauce
1/2   cup (125 mL) cider vinegar
1/2   cup (125 mL) pineapple juice
1/2   cup (125 mL) sugar
1   medium onion, thinly sliced,
        separated into rings
1   clove garlic, minced
1   teaspoon (5 mL) pared, grated
        fresh ginger root or 1/4
        teaspoon (1 mL) ground
        ginger
1/4   teaspoon (1 mL) ground cloves
1   tablespoon (15 mL) sesame
        seeds

These chunky spareribs are cooked in a ginger-scented soy sauce. Good accompaniments are steamed rice and a fresh pineapple salad with a creamy dressing.

1. Soak top and bottom of 3¹/4-quart (3.25 L) clay cooker in water about 15 minutes; drain.

2. Place spareribs, fat side up, in cooker.

3. Place covered cooker in cold oven. Set oven at 425°F (220°C). Bake 1¹/2 hours; pour off and discard drippings.

4. While spareribs are baking, heat remaining ingredients except sesame seeds in medium saucepan, stirring constantly, until sugar dissolves and mixture bubbles; reduce heat. Simmer covered 10 minutes.

5. Pour about half the sauce over spareribs. Bake covered, adding remaining sauce in two or three additions, until meat is tender and brown, about 1 hour.

6. Sprinkle spareribs with sesame seeds. Bake uncovered until seeds are light brown, 5 to 10 minutes.

Perfect Poultry

If ever a food and a cooking utensil were made for each other, that combination must be the clay cooker and poultry. Consider the ideal roast bird—golden and crisp-skinned, juicy and moist within. Cooking in clay is the perfect means of achieving this.

Clay cookers can be found that will hold poultry of almost any size, up to a 12- to 14-pound (5.5 to 6.4 kg) turkey. In a small clay cooker, such as one of 2-quart (2 L) capacity, you can roast a Rock Cornish game hen or a small chicken. A versatile 3¼-quart (3.25 L) clay cooker accommodates a whole chicken weighing as much as 6 pounds (2700 g), an average-size duckling or two Cornish hens. A very large clay cooker of nearly 5-quart (5 L) capacity is big enough for a holiday turkey or even four Cornish hens for a company dinner.

Roasting a whole bird in a clay cooker is simpler and neater than the conventional open-roasting process. The cooker is covered during all but the last 10 to 15 minutes in the oven. That means that your oven is virtually free from messy splattering. It isn't necessary to use a roasting rack in a clay cooker that has a ridged bottom. And the relatively high oven temperature gets the bird cooked somewhat faster than the recommended times found on charts for standard roasting of poultry.

You may find that when you roast a whole bird that nearly fills the clay cooker, the skin tends to stick to the sides it touches. Lining the clay cooker with baking parchment paper will help to keep the skin intact.

Certainly clay cooking should not be limited to roasting poultry whole, as superbly as it does that. You can also cook chicken or turkey pieces in flavorful sauces, in the style of many different cuisines from around the world. As with meats, poultry cooked by this method requires no browning before going into the clay cooker. That means you can just about omit the use of any sort of fat or cooking oil—a useful saving when you are counting calories.

It is in this sort of dish that the flavor magic of clay cooking becomes most obvious. Even simple seasonings seem to blend more harmoniously with the natural flavors of chicken or other poultry to make your cooking more interesting than ever before.

Wedding Chicken from Crete

Makes 5 to 6 servings

1   small onion, finely chopped
2   tablespoons (30 mL) olive oil
     or vegetable oil
2/3 cup (about 160 mL) uncooked
     long-grain white rice
3   tablespoons (45 mL) pine nuts
     or slivered almonds
1   lemon
1¼   cups (310 mL) regular-strength
     chicken broth, canned or
     homemade
1   clove garlic, minced
2   tablespoons (30 mL) dried
     currants
½   teaspoon (2 mL) salt
¼   teaspoon (1 mL) ground
     cinnamon
1   whole large frying chicken
     (3¾ to 4 pounds or 1600 to
     1800 g)
¼   pound (115 g) mushrooms,
     sliced
¼   teaspoon (1 mL) dried
     rosemary leaves, crumbled

A lemony rice stuffing with currants and pine nuts fills this elegant stuffed chicken, roasted with mushrooms and lemon juice. All you need to complete this choice dish is a simple green vegetable, such as lightly cooked sliced zucchini.

1. Sauté onion in oil in medium skillet until soft but not brown. Stir in rice and pine nuts; cook until light brown. Grate lemon rind; squeeze juice and reserve. Stir chicken broth, garlic, currants, salt, cinnamon and lemon rind into rice. Cook covered over low heat 20 minutes (rice will be slightly chewy).

2. Soak top and bottom of 3¼-quart (3.25 L) clay cooker in water about 15 minutes; drain.

3. Rinse chicken and pat dry, reserving neck and giblets for other use. Fill cavity with rice mixture. Place chicken, breast side up, in cooker. Arrange mushrooms around chicken. Drizzle reserved lemon juice over chicken and mushrooms; sprinkle with rosemary.

4. Place covered cooker in cold oven. Set oven at 475°F (250°C). Bake until chicken is tender and juices run clear when thigh is pierced, about 1¼ hours. If necessary, remove cover and bake until chicken is crisp and brown, 5 to 10 minutes.

5. Carve chicken; serve with mushrooms, cooking liquid and rice stuffing.

Creamy Paprika Chicken

Makes 4 servings

1   frying chicken (3 to 3½ pounds
     or 1350 to 1600 g), cut into
     quarters
     Flour
2   medium onions, finely chopped
1   clove garlic, minced
2   teaspoons (10 mL) sweet
     Hungarian paprika
1   teaspoon (5 mL) salt
⅛   teaspoon (0.5 mL) white
     pepper
⅓   cup (80 mL) dry white wine
1   cup (250 mL) sour cream
     Minced fresh parsley

Noodles are appetizing with paprika-seasoned chicken quarters cooked in wine with an abundance of onions. Stir in sour cream at the end to complete the sauce.

1. Soak top and bottom of 3¼-quart (3.25 L) clay cooker in water about 15 minutes; drain.

2. Coat chicken lightly with flour, tapping to remove excess. Place onions and garlic in cooker; cover with chicken quarters, skin sides up. Sprinkle evenly with paprika, salt and pepper. Pour in wine.

3. Place covered cooker in cold oven. Set oven at 450°F (230°C). Bake until chicken is tender and brown, about 1¼ hours. Stir in sour cream. Turn off oven. Cover chicken and return to oven until sauce is hot, 5 to 10 minutes.

4. Garnish with parsley.

Gita's Curried Chicken

Makes 6 servings

1 large onion, finely chopped
2 tablespoons (30 mL) vegetable oil
1 piece fresh ginger root, 1-inch (2.5 cm) pared, cut into slivers, or 1/2 teaspoon (2 mL) ground ginger
1/3 cup (80 mL) tomato juice
1 clove garlic, minced
1 teaspoon (5 mL) salt
1 teaspoon (5 mL) ground coriander
1 teaspoon (5 mL) ground cumin
1/2 teaspoon (2 mL) paprika
1/2 teaspoon (2 mL) ground turmeric
1/8 to 1/4 teaspoon (0.5 to 1 mL) cayenne pepper
1/8 teaspoon (0.5 mL) ground cinnamon
Pinch ground cloves
1 small bay leaf
3 pounds (1350 g) chicken pieces, skinned

If you have never mixed your own curry powder — combining familiar sweet and savory spices as Indian cooks do — the flavor of this simple but quite authentic curried chicken may surprise you. Skinning the chicken before cooking enables the spicy flavors to permeate it.

1. Soak top and bottom of 2- to 3 1/4-quart (2 to 3.25 L) clay cooker in water about 15 minutes; drain.

2. Sauté onion in oil in medium skillet just until beginning to brown; reduce heat. Stir in ginger; cook, stirring constantly, about 2 minutes. Stir in remaining ingredients except chicken. Remove from heat.

3. Place chicken pieces in cooker. Add onion mixture; mix.

4. Place covered cooker in cold oven. Set oven at 450°F (230°C). Bake, stirring once or twice, until chicken is tender, about 1 hour.

5. To serve, spoon sauce over chicken.

Chicken with Cheddar and Green Chiles

Makes 6 servings

3 pounds (1350 g) meaty chicken pieces
2 tablespoons (30 mL) flour
2 teaspoons (10 mL) chili powder
1 teaspoon (5 mL) salt
1/2 teaspoon (2 mL) ground cumin
1 rib celery, finely chopped
1 small onion, finely chopped
1 clove garlic, minced
1 can (4 ounces or 115 g) diced green chiles
1/2 cup (125 mL) regular-strength chicken broth, canned or homemade
1/2 cup (125 mL) sour cream
1 cup (250 mL) shredded Cheddar cheese

For those who enjoy Mexican food, here is a zippy way to serve chicken from a clay cooker in a vivid south-of-the-border sauce. Try it with plain white rice.

1. Soak top and bottom of 3 1/4-quart (3.25 L) clay cooker in water about 15 minutes; drain.

2. Coat chicken pieces with mixture of flour, chili powder, salt and cumin. Combine celery, onion and garlic in cooker. Top with chicken and green chiles. Pour in chicken broth.

3. Place covered cooker in cold oven. Set oven at 450°F (230°C). Bake, stirring once or twice, until chicken is tender and brown, about 1 1/4 hours.

4. Remove chicken from cooker. Skim and discard fat from cooking liquid in cooker. Stir sour cream into cooking liquid until smooth. Return chicken to sauce. Sprinkle with cheese. Bake until cheese melts and browns, about 10 minutes.

Roast Duckling with Fresh Pineapple

1   **small fresh pineapple**
1   **duckling (3³/4 to 4 pounds or
     1600 to 1800 g), giblets and
     neck reserved**
     Salt
1   **tablespoon (15 mL) butter or
     margarine**
2   **cups (500 mL) water**
2   **tablespoons (30 mL) tomato
     paste**
¹/4   **teaspoon (1 mL) whole allspice**
¹/2   **teaspoon (2 mL) salt**
     Pinch white pepper
¹/4   **cup (60 mL) tarragon vinegar**
¹/3   **cup (80 mL) dry white wine**
2   **teaspoons (10 mL) cornstarch**
1   **tablespoon (15 mL) water**
¹/4   **cup (60 mL) orange-flavored
     liqueur**

One great advantage of cooking duck in a clay cooker is that it is covered, containing the fat neatly within the cooker rather than allowing it to spurt all over your oven. When you roast a duckling in a clay cooker, at 30-minute intervals pierce it all over with a fork to permit the fat to drain. Use a baster to remove it as it accumulates in the cooker (reserve the fat and drippings for sauce). The result: crisp-skinned, well browned duckling with juicy meat.

1. The day before cooking duckling, cut top from pineapple and pare. Cut pineapple crosswise into ¹/2-inch (1.5 cm) slices. Remove and discard core from each slice. Place slices in bowl; refrigerate covered overnight.

2. Soak top and bottom of 3¹/4-quart (3.25 L) clay cooker in water about 15 minutes; drain.

3. Rinse duckling and pat dry, reserving giblets and neck for sauce. Sprinkle duckling inside and out with salt; close cavity with skewer. Place duckling, breast side up, in cooker.

4. Place covered cooker in cold oven. Set oven at 425°F (220°C). Bake, piercing skin in several places with fork at 30-minute intervals, until duckling is crisp and brown, 1³/4 to 2 hours. If necessary, remove cover and bake until crisp and brown, 10 to 15 minutes.

5. Sauté neck and giblets in butter in large saucepan until browned on all sides. Stir in 2 cups (500 mL) water, the tomato paste, allspice, ¹/2 teaspoon (2 mL) salt and the pepper. Heat to boiling; reduce heat. Simmer covered 30 minutes. Remove cover, simmer 30 minutes.

6. Drain juice from pineapple slices into small saucepan; add vinegar. Boil gently until liquid turns caramel colored. Add wine; cook until reduced by about half.

7. Strain giblet mixture and discard giblets and neck. Mix cornstarch and 1 tablespoon (15 mL) water; stir into broth. Stir in pineapple juice mixture. Cook, stirring constantly, until thickened and clear; keep warm.

8. Remove duckling from clay cooker and keep warm; pour off cooking liquid. Skim fat, reserving 1 tablespoon (15 mL). Add cooking liquid to sauce.

9. Cut pineapple slices into halves. Sauté pineapple slices lightly in reserved fat in medium skillet; remove from heat. Sprinkle with liqueur and ignite. Stir pan juices into sauce.

10. Cut duckling into quarters; arrange on warm platter. Surround with pineapple slices. Spoon a little of the sauce over duckling and pineapple. Serve with remaining sauce.

Baked Chicken with Artichokes

¹/₄   pound (115 g) mushrooms,
      thinly sliced
1   small onion, finely chopped
1   clove garlic, finely chopped
3   pounds (1350 g) meaty chicken
      pieces
2   tablespoons (30 mL) flour
1¹/₂ teaspoons (7 mL) salt
¹/₂   teaspoon (2 mL) paprika
¹/₄   teaspoon (1 mL) dried
      rosemary leaves, crumbled
¹/₈   teaspoon (0.5 mL) white
      pepper
¹/₂   cup (125 mL) regular-strength
      chicken broth, canned or
      homemade
¹/₄   cup (60 mL) dry sherry
1   can (14 ounces or about 400 g)
      artichoke hearts, drained

Chicken pieces bake atop savory vegetables to make a distinctive main dish that is a favorite in San Francisco's Italian restaurants.

1. Soak top and bottom of 3¹/₄-quart (3.25 L) clay cooker in water about 15 minutes; drain.

2. Place mushrooms, onion and garlic in cooker. Coat chicken pieces with mixture of flour, salt, paprika, rosemary and pepper. Arrange chicken pieces, skin sides up, in even layer over vegetables. Pour in chicken broth and sherry.

3. Place covered cooker in cold oven. Set oven at 450°F (230°C). Bake just until chicken is tender, about 1 hour. Stir in artichoke hearts gently. Bake covered until artichokes are hot, 8 to 10 minutes.

4. Remove cover; bake until chicken is crisp and brown, 5 to 10 minutes.

Cornish Hens in Vinegar

1   small onion, finely chopped
4   Rock Cornish game hens (each
      20 to 24 ounces or 575 to
      675 g)
      Salt
      White pepper
1   can (8 ounces or 225 g) tomato
      sauce
2   cloves garlic, minced
3   tablespoons (45 mL) red wine
      vinegar
¹/₂   teaspoon (2 mL) sugar
¹/₄   teaspoon (1 mL) dried thyme
      leaves, crumbled
1   bay leaf
1   teaspoon (5 mL) cornstarch
1   tablespoon (15 mL) water
      Minced fresh parsley

A gleaming crimson sauce embellishes Cornish hens cooked in a style favored by French chefs. Complete the menu with Potatoes Anna (see Index for page number) and fresh leaf spinach.

1. Soak top and bottom of 4³/₄-quart (4.75 L) clay cooker in water about 15 minutes; drain.

2. Place onions in cooker. Rinse hens and pat dry, reserving giblets for other use. Sprinkle hens, inside and out, with salt and pepper. Place hens, breast sides up, in cooker. Mix tomato sauce, garlic, vinegar, sugar and thyme; pour into cooker. Insert bay leaf near center.

3. Place covered cooker in cold oven. Set oven at 475°F (250°C). Bake, stirring and basting with sauce once or twice, until hens are tender and brown, about 1¹/₂ hours.

4. Remove hens to warm serving platter; keep warm. Skim and discard fat from cooking liquid. Strain into medium skillet. Mix cornstarch and water; stir into skillet. Heat to boiling; cook, stirring constantly, until thickened and clear. Pour sauce over hens; garnish with parsley.

Makes 8 servings

Tangy Turkey Loaf

1   medium onion, finely chopped
1 1/2 tablespoons (22 mL) butter or
          margarine
2   eggs
1/3   cup (80 mL) milk
2   tablespoons (30 mL) prepared
          horseradish
3   tablespoons (45 mL) chili
          sauce
1   clove garlic, minced
1/2   teaspoon (2 mL) salt
1/2   cup (125 mL) finely crushed
          saltine crackers
2   pounds (900 g) ground turkey
1/2   pound (225 g) ground ham
1/4   cup (60 mL) minced fresh
          parsley
1/2   cup (125 mL) sour cream
2   tablespoons (30 mL) drained
          capers

Ground turkey makes a less costly substitute for ground veal. With ground ham, it also makes a moist, flavorful meat loaf with a stylish pink color.

1. Soak top and bottom of 2-quart (2 L) clay cooker in water about 15 minutes; drain.

2. Sauté onion in butter until soft but not brown. Beat eggs slightly in large bowl; stir in milk, horseradish, chili sauce, garlic and salt. Add cracker crumbs and let stand 1 minute. Stir in sautéed onions, the turkey, ham and parsley. Pat mixture into cooker.

3. Place covered cooker in cold oven. Set oven at 450°F (230°C). Bake until brown and juices run clear when knife is inserted in center, about 1 1/4 hours.

4. Let stand covered about 5 minutes. Combine sour cream and capers. Loosen edges of turkey loaf and invert onto warm serving platter. Slice turkey loaf and spoon sauce over slices.

Makes 4 servings

Chicken Braised with Cabbage

1   large onion, finely chopped
2   cloves garlic, minced
1   bay leaf
1   frying chicken (3 to 3 1/2
          pounds or 1350 to 1600 g),
          cut into quarters
1   tablespoon (15 mL) Dijon-style
          mustard
1/4   teaspoon (1 mL) ground
          nutmeg
1/4   cup (60 mL) dry white wine
1   small head (about 1 1/2 pounds
          or 675 g) green cabbage, cut
          into quarters
1/2   teaspoon (2 mL) salt
       Pinch white pepper

With chicken and vegetables cooked together, this entrée is not only convenient but also economical. Good accompaniments are a crusty bread and parsley-buttered carrots.

1. Soak top and bottom of 3 1/4-quart (3.25 L) clay cooker in water about 15 minutes; drain.

2. Place onion, garlic and bay leaf in cooker. Cover with chicken quarters, skin sides up. Spread chicken evenly with mustard; sprinkle with nutmeg. Pour in wine.

3. Place covered cooker in cold oven. Set oven at 475°F (250°C). Bake until chicken is almost tender, about 45 minutes. Remove chicken. Place cabbage wedges in cooker. Sprinkle with salt and pepper. Place chicken quarters over cabbage wedges. Bake covered until cabbage is crisp-tender, 20 to 25 minutes.

4. Remove cover; bake until chicken is crisp and brown, 5 to 10 minutes. Remove chicken and cabbage to serving platter; spoon a little of the cooking liquid over chicken and cabbage.

Chicken Saltimbocca

Makes 4 to 6 servings

3   **whole chicken breasts (about 3 pounds or 1350 g), boned, skinned, cut into halves**

6   **thin slices prosciutto or boiled ham**

6   **thin slices Swiss cheese**
     Flour

1/2   **pound (225 g) mushrooms, sliced**

1/8   **teaspoon (0.5 mL) ground nutmeg**

1/2   **cup (125 mL) regular-strength chicken broth, canned or homemade**

1/3   **cup (80 mL) Marsala wine**

1/4   **cup (60 mL) grated Parmesan cheese**

2   **teaspoons (10 mL) cornstarch**

1   **tablespoon (15 mL) water**

This Italian dish usually involves a certain amount of last-minute cooking. Baking the ham and cheese-stuffed rolls of boneless chicken breasts in a clay cooker, however, simplifies its preparation considerably.

1. Soak top and bottom of 2-quart (2 L) clay cooker in water about 15 minutes; drain.

2. Place chicken breasts between sheets of waxed paper; pound, using the flat side of a meat mallet, until slightly flattened. Place 1 slice of prosciutto and 1 slice cheese on boned side of each breast. Tuck in sides and roll up. Secure with wooden picks or small metal skewers. Lightly coat chicken rolls with flour.

3. Place mushrooms in cooker. Top with single layer of chicken rolls. Sprinkle with nutmeg. Pour in broth and Marsala. Sprinkle with Parmesan cheese.

4. Place covered cooker in cold oven. Set oven at 425°F (220°C). Bake until chicken is tender and light brown, about 1 hour. Remove chicken breasts to warm serving bowl; keep warm.

5. Pour cooking liquid and mushrooms into a medium skillet. Mix cornstarch and water; stir into skillet. Heat to boiling, stirring constantly. Cook until thickened and clear. Pour mushroom sauce over chicken.

Cheese-Stuffed Cornish Hens

Makes 2 servings

2   **Rock Cornish game hens (each 20 to 24 ounces or 575 to 675 g)**
     Salt
     White pepper
     Nutmeg

1   **package (4 ounces or 115 g) garlic-and-herb flavored cream cheese**

2   **tablespoons (30 mL) butter or margarine, melted**

1   **small loaf brown-and-serve French bread**
     Watercress

As these hens bake the savory cheese inside melts and mingles with the cooking juices to become a luscious sauce. Use French bread to soak up all the goodness!

1. Soak top and bottom of 3 1/4-quart (3.25 L) clay cooker in water about 15 minutes; drain.

2. Rinse hens and pat dry, reserving giblets for other use. Sprinkle hens with salt, pepper and nutmeg. Place half of cheese inside each hen. Place hens, breast sides up, in cooker. Drizzle with melted butter.

3. Place covered cooker in cold oven. Set oven at 450°F (230°C). Bake until hens are tender and light brown, about 1 1/4 hours. Remove cover; bake until brown about 10 minutes. At the same time, heat bread in oven until hot and brown, about 10 minutes.

4. Spoon cooking juices over hens. Garnish with watercress. Serve with bread.

Makes 8 to 10 servings

Mushroom-Stuffed Turkey Breast

Mushroom Purée (recipe follows)
1   turkey breast (4¹/2 to 5 pounds or 1800 to 2250 g)
1   tablespoon (15 mL) soft butter or margarine
¹/2 teaspoon (2 mL) salt
¹/8 teaspoon (0.5 mL) white pepper
¹/8 teaspoon (0.5 mL) ground nutmeg
¹/4 cup (60 mL) Madeira or sherry wine
6   thin slices aged Gruyère or Swiss cheese
2   teaspoons (10 mL) cornstarch
1   tablespoon (15 mL) water

A boned turkey breast can be transformed into a handsome roast for an elegant company dinner. Inside is a moist purée of mushrooms and ham, and the surface of the turkey is glazed with melted cheese. The Broccoli au Gratin (see Index for page number) complements this main dish tastefully.

1. Soak top and bottom of 3¹/4-quart (3.25 L) clay cooker in water about 15 minutes; drain.

2. Make Mushroom Purée.

3. Bone and skin turkey breast. Place 1 breast half, boned side up, on board. Spread evenly with Mushroom Purée, leaving 1-inch (2.5 cm) border on all sides. Cover with remaining breast half, boned side down. Sew edges together with white string. Place in cooker. Spread with butter; sprinkle with salt, pepper and nutmeg. Pour in Madeira.

4. Place covered cooker in cold oven. Set oven at 425°F (220°C). Bake until turkey is light brown and juices run clear when a small knife is inserted in center, about 1¹/2 hours.

5. Pour cooking liquid into medium saucepan. Arrange cheese slices evenly over turkey roll. Bake uncovered until cheese melts and browns lightly, about 10 minutes.

6. Mix cornstarch and water; stir into cooking liquid. Heat to boiling; cook, stirring constantly, until thickened and clear. Remove string and slice turkey breast. Spoon sauce over slices.

Makes about 1 cup (250 mL)

Mushroom Purée

¹/2 pound (225 g) mushrooms, coarsely chopped
1¹/2 tablespoons (22 mL) lemon juice
2   tablespoons (30 mL) butter or margarine
¹/4 cup (60 mL) ground ham
¹/4 teaspoon (1 mL) salt
¹/2 cup (125 mL) whipping cream

1. Process mushrooms and lemon juice in food processor until smooth.

2. Heat butter in medium skillet. Add mushroom purée and ham. Cook and stir about 3 minutes; add salt and cream. Cook over medium-high heat, stirring constantly, until most of the liquid has evaporated. Purée should be thick and of spreading consistency.

Makes 6 servings

Coq au Vin

3 pounds (1350 g) meaty chicken pieces
1 teaspoon (5 mL) fines herbes
1 teaspoon (5 mL) salt
1/8 teaspoon (0.5 mL) pepper
1 clove garlic, minced
1 medium onion, finely chopped
1 carrot, pared, shredded
1/2 cup (about 125 mL) julienne-cut ham strips
1 bay leaf
1 1/2 cups (375 mL) dry red wine
1/2 pound (225 g) mushrooms, cut into quarters
4 tablespoons (60 mL) butter or margarine
2 medium onions, each cut into 6 wedges
1/4 cup (60 mL) Armagnac or other brandy
1 tablespoon (15 mL) flour
   Minced fresh parsley

Marinating chicken pieces intensifies the flavor of this traditional French dish. Serve the chicken and sauce with tiny, red-skinned new potatoes.

1. Place chicken pieces in shallow bowl. Sprinkle with fines herbes, salt, pepper and garlic. Stir in chopped onion, the carrot, ham and bay leaf. Pour in wine. Refrigerate covered, turning once or twice, 8 hours or overnight.

2. Soak top and bottom of 3 1/4-quart (3.25 L) clay cooker in water about 15 minutes; drain.

3. Place chicken, vegetables and marinade in cooker. Sauté mushrooms in 2 tablespoons (30 mL) of the butter until light brown; add to chicken. Sauté onion wedges in 1 tablespoon (15 mL) of the butter until brown; add to chicken. Warm Armagnac slightly; ignite and pour flaming over chicken.

4. Place covered cooker in cold oven. Set oven at 450°F (230°C). Bake, stirring once or twice, until chicken is tender and brown, 1 1/4 to 1 1/2 hours.

5. Pour off cooking liquid; skim and discard fat. Turn off oven; return uncovered cooker to oven. Transfer cooking liquid to large skillet. Mix remaining butter with flour until smooth; stir into cooking liquid. Heat to boiling; cook, stirring constantly, until thickened and clear, 5 to 8 minutes. Pour sauce over chicken. Garnish with parsley.

Makes 4 servings

Tandoori Chicken

2 whole small frying chickens (each 2 to 2 1/2 pounds or 900 to 1125 g)
2 tablespoons (30 mL) lime or lemon juice
2 teaspoons (10 mL) salt
2/3 cup (160 mL) plain yogurt
2 cloves garlic, minced
2 teaspoons (10 mL) pared grated fresh ginger root or 1/2 teaspoon (2 mL) ground ginger
1 teaspoon (5 mL) ground cumin
1 teaspoon (5 mL) ground coriander

A clay cooker makes a reasonable stand-in for the special Indian charcoal-fired clay oven called a tandoor, which is used for cooking authentic tandoori chicken. The chicken is skinned to allow the spicy flavors of its yogurt marinade to penetrate.

As prepared in India tandoori chicken may have a red-gold color caused in part by the use of a red dye called cochineal in the marinade. You may wish to use red food coloring to simulate this, but it is certainly not necessary to the success of the dish.

1. One to two days before cooking chickens, remove and discard skin from chickens; reserve necks and giblets for other use. Pierce breasts, thighs and legs in several places with fork. Place chickens in shallow glass baking dish; spoon on lime juice slowly. Sprinkle evenly with salt.

TANDOORI CHICKEN, continued

¹/₄ teaspoon (1 mL) cayenne
   pepper
¹/₄ teaspoon (1 mL) red food color,
   if desired
¹/₈ teaspoon (0.5 mL) powdered
   saffron or saffron threads
   Green onions
   Lime or lemon wedges
   Fresh coriander sprigs
   (Chinese parsley)
   Radishes

2. Mix yogurt, garlic, ginger, cumin, coriander, cayenne, food color and saffron. Spread yogurt mixture evenly over chicken. Cover lightly. Refrigerate 1 to 2 days.

3. Soak top and bottom of 3¹/₄- to 4³/₄-quart (3.25 to 4.75 L) clay cooker in water about 15 minutes; drain.

4. Place chickens, breast sides up, in cooker; spoon any remaining marinade over chickens.

5. Place covered cooker in cold oven. Set oven at 475°F (250°C). Bake until chicken is tender and juices run clear when thigh is pierced, about 1 hour. Remove cover; bake until coating is crusty and brown, 5 to 10 minutes.

6. Cut chickens in half; garnish with green onions, lime wedges, coriander sprigs and radishes.

Makes 6 servings

Cashew Chicken

¹/₂ pound (225 g) mushrooms,
   thinly sliced
1 can (8 ounces or 225 g) sliced
   bamboo shoots, drained
3 whole chicken breasts (about 3
   pounds or 1350 g), boned,
   skinned, cut into 1-inch (2.5
   cm) pieces
²/₃ cup (160 mL) regular-strength
   chicken broth, canned or
   homemade
2 tablespoons (30 mL)
   cornstarch
¹/₄ cup (60 mL) soy sauce
¹/₂ teaspoon (2 mL) sugar
¹/₂ teaspoon (2 mL) salt
¹/₄ teaspoon (1 mL) ground ginger
³/₄ cup (180 mL) dry-roasted
   cashews
1 tablespoon (15 mL) vegetable
   oil
4 green onions with tops, cut into
   1-inch (2.5 cm) pieces,
   slivered
1 package (6 ounces or 170 g)
   frozen Chinese pea pods,
   thawed, drained

You may be surprised at how well this Chinese dish, usually stir-fried, can be prepared in a clay cooker entirely in the oven. One advantage is that the final preparation timing can be so much more relaxed.

1. Soak top and bottom of 2- to 3¹/₄-quart (2 to 3.25 L) clay cooker in water about 15 minutes; drain.

2. Spread mushrooms and bamboo shoots in cooker. Cover with chicken pieces. Stir chicken broth gradually into cornstarch in small bowl; stir in soy sauce, sugar, salt and ginger. Pour over chicken.

3. Place covered cooker in cold oven. Set oven at 400°F (200°C). Bake, stirring two or three times, until chicken is tender, 45 to 50 minutes.

4. Sauté cashews in oil in small skillet until brown.

5. Stir green onions and pea pods gently into chicken. Turn off oven. Cover cooker and return to oven until pea pods are hot, 5 to 10 minutes. Sprinkle with cashews.

Spanish Chicken with Rice

Makes 4 servings

1   cup (250 mL) uncooked long-
       grain white rice
1   medium onion, finely chopped
1   clove garlic, minced
1   linguica or chorizo sausage (6
       to 8 ounces or about 225 g),
       casing removed, crumbled
1   jar (2 ounces or 60 g) sliced
       pimiento, undrained
1/8 teaspoon (0.5 mL) dried
       saffron threads or powdered
       saffron
1   can (13 3/4 ounces or 400 g)
       regular-strength chicken
       broth
1   frying chicken (about 3 pounds
       or 1350 g), cut into quarters
    Salt
    Seasoned pepper
1/2 cup (125 mL) frozen peas,
       thawed

Using a clay cooker enables you to prepare this colorful meal-in-one (called arroz con pollo) *in the oven — as easy a festive dinner as can be imagined. Serve it with warm French bread and a green salad with orange slices.*

1. Soak top and bottom of 3 1/4-quart (3.25 L) clay cooker in water about 15 minutes; drain.

2. Combine rice, onion, garlic, sausage, pimiento and saffron in cooker. Pour in chicken broth. Arrange chicken quarters, skin sides up, over rice mixture. Sprinkle chicken with salt and pepper.

3. Place covered cooker in cold oven. Set oven at 475°F (250°C). Bake until chicken is tender, about 1 hour.

4. Remove chicken and stir in peas; return chicken to cooker. Bake uncovered until chicken is crisp and brown, about 10 minutes.

Chicken with Fresh Figs

Makes 4 servings

4   chicken legs with thighs,
       (about 3 pounds or 1350 g)
1/2 teaspoon (2 mL) salt
1/8 teaspoon (0.5 mL) ground
       mace or nutmeg
8   fresh figs, cut crosswise into
       1/4-inch (0.5 cm) slices
1/3 cup (80 mL) Madeira wine
1/3 cup (80 mL) whipping cream
    Watercress

Sometimes it is worth saving a recipe until the ingredients are in season. Here is a good example. Fresh figs are so much more delicate than their dried counterparts that their brief late summer season is an event. Cooked with chicken, they give its cream sauce an appealing rosy tinge.

1. Soak top and bottom of 2-quart (2 L) clay cooker in water about 15 minutes; drain.

2. Place chicken legs, skin sides up, in cooker. Sprinkle with salt and mace. Add figs. Pour in Madeira.

3. Place covered cooker in cold oven. Set oven at 475°F (250°C). Bake until chicken is tender, about 50 minutes. Remove cover; bake until chicken is brown, about 10 minutes.

4. Pour cooking liquid into medium skillet. Cover cooker to keep chicken warm. Add cream to cooking liquid. Heat to boiling; cook, stirring occasionally, until slightly thickened. Pour sauce over chicken. Garnish with watercress.

Peppered Roast Duckling

Makes 4 servings

1 duckling (3³/4 to 4 pounds or
  1600 to 1800 g)
  Salt
3 tablespoons (45 mL) black
  peppercorns
  Watercress

A generous coating of coarsely ground pepper encrusts duckling with robust flavor, giving the crisp skin an added crunch. Cooking seems to gentle the pepper somewhat, lessening its bite. Those who enjoy pepper steak will appreciate this similar treatment of duck. Accompany it with a light, fruity red wine such as a young Beaujolais.

1. Soak top and bottom of 3¹/4-quart (3.25 L) clay cooker in water about 15 minutes; drain.

2. Rinse duckling and pat dry, reserving giblets for other use. Sprinkle cavity with salt. Process peppercorns in small blender jar until coarsely ground. (Or use coarse peppermill or mortar and pestle.) Cover duckling with pepper, patting firmly onto skin. Place duckling, breast side up, in cooker.

3. Place covered cooker in cold oven. Set oven at 425°F (220°C). Bake, piercing skin in several places with fork every 30 minutes, until duckling is well browned, 1³/4 hours to 2 hours. Spoon off and discard fat. Bake uncovered until crisp, 10 to 15 minutes.

4. Cut duckling into quarters; garnish with watercress.

Honey Glazed Cornish Hens with Rice Stuffing

Makes 4 servings

1 package (6 ounces or 170 g)
  white-and-wild rice mix
¹/3 cup (80 mL) slivered almonds
4 Rock Cornish game hens (each
  20 to 24 ounces or 575 to
  675 g)
  Salt
2 tablespoons (30 mL) honey
1 tablespoon (15 mL) butter or
  margarine
1 teaspoon (5 mL) dry mustard
¹/4 teaspoon (1 mL) curry powder
¹/8 teaspoon (0.5 mL) ground
  ginger

Festive and attractive, Cornish hens plump with an almond-studded white and wild rice stuffing, making a delicious center of attention for a company dinner.

1. Soak top and bottom of 4³/4-quart (4.75 L) clay cooker in water about 15 minutes; drain.

2. Cook rice mix according to package directions, using ¹/4 (60 mL) cup less water; cook uncovered during last 5 minutes. Stir in almonds.

3. Rinse hens and pat dry, reserving giblets for other use. Sprinkle hens inside and out with salt. Fill cavities with rice stuffing; close openings with small skewers. Place hens, breast sides up, in cooker.

4. Place covered cooker in cold oven. Set oven at 475°F (250°C). Bake until hens are tender and legs move easily, about 1¹/4 hours.

5. Heat honey, butter, mustard, curry powder and ginger in small saucepan stirring until melted and bubbly. Brush hens with honey glaze. Bake uncovered until shiny and dark brown, 10 to 15 minutes. Remove hens to serving platter. Skim and discard fat from cooking liquid; spoon over hens.

Chicken Tarragon

Makes 4 servings

1   frying chicken (3 to 3¹/₄ pounds or 1350 to 1450 g), cut into quarters
2   tablespoons (30 mL) lemon juice
1   tablespoon (15 mL) tarragon vinegar
1   teaspoon (5 mL) dried tarragon leaves
1   teaspoon (5 mL) salt
        Pinch white pepper
2   shallots, finely chopped, or 2 tablespoons (30 mL) finely chopped mild onion
¹/₂   cup (125 mL) regular-strength chicken broth, canned or homemade
¹/₂   cup (125 mL) whipping cream

A tart tarragon and cream sauce distinguishes chicken quarters baked in a clay cooker to achieve an elegant French dish. Serve it with new potatoes baked or steamed in their jackets.

1. Soak top and bottom of 3¹/₄-quart (3.25 L) clay cooker in water about 15 minutes; drain.

2. Place chicken quarters, skin sides up, in clay cooker. Drizzle with lemon juice and vinegar. Sprinkle with tarragon, salt, pepper and shallots. Pour in chicken broth.

3. Place covered cooker in cold oven. Set oven at 450°F (230°C). Bake until chicken is tender and light brown, about 1¹/₄ hours.

4. Pour cooking liquid into medium skillet. Add whipping cream to cooking liquid. Heat to boiling; cook, stirring occasionally, until slightly thickened. Pour over chicken.

Basque Chicken

Makes 4 servings

1   large green pepper, cut into quarters, cut crosswise into thin strips
2   medium onions, thinly sliced, separated into rings
¹/₄   pound (115 g) mushrooms, thinly sliced
2   cloves garlic, minced
1   frying chicken (3 to 3¹/₂ pounds or 1350 to 1600 g), cut into quarters
1   teaspoon (5 mL) salt
        Pinch freshly ground black pepper
¹/₄   teaspoon (1 mL) cayenne pepper
1   can (8 ounces or 225 g) tomato sauce
¹/₄   cup (60 mL) dry white wine
2   teaspoons (10 mL) cornstarch
1   tablespoon (15 mL) water

In the mountainous Southwest of France, Basque heritage dictates chicken be cooked in a piquant tomato sauce with green pepper, garlic and mushrooms. This dish teams well with rice.

1. Soak top and bottom of 3¹/₄-quart (3.25 L) clay cooker in water about 15 minutes; drain.

2. Place green pepper, onions, mushrooms and garlic in cooker. Place chicken quarters, skin sides up, over vegetables. Sprinkle with salt and black and cayenne peppers. Mix tomato sauce and wine; pour into cooker.

3. Place covered cooker in cold oven. Set oven at 450°F (230°C). Bake until chicken is tender and light brown, about 1¹/₄ hours. Remove chicken pieces to warm serving bowl; keep warm.

4. Pour cooking liquid with vegetables into a medium skillet. Mix cornstarch and water; stir into skillet. Heat to boiling; cook, stirring constantly, until thickened and clear. Pour sauce and vegetables over chicken.

Cornish Hens with Grapes

Makes 2 servings

2	Rock Cornish game hens, (each 20 to 24 ounces or 575 to 675 g)
	Salt
	White pepper
6	tablespoons (90 mL) port wine
1	tablespoon (15 mL) butter or margarine
1/8	teaspoon (0.5 mL) ground nutmeg
1	cup (250 mL) red grapes, cut into halves, seeded
1/3	cup (80 mL) whipping cream

For that special little candlelight dinner for two, serve Cornish hens in a delicate cream sauce with red grapes. Accompany with fruity white wine.

1. Soak top and bottom of 3 1/4-quart (3.25 L) clay cooker in water about 15 minutes; drain.

2. Rinse hens and pat dry, reserving giblets for other use. Sprinkle hens inside and out, with salt and pepper. Place breasts sides up in cooker. Heat 2 tablespoons (30 mL) port, the butter and nutmeg; drizzle butter mixture over hens.

3. Place covered cooker in cold oven. Set oven at 450°F (230°C). Bake, brushing once or twice with cooking liquid, until hens are tender and light brown and legs move easily, about 1 1/4 hours. Remove cover, bake until dark brown, 5 to 10 minutes.

4. Remove hens to warm serving platter; keep warm. Pour cooking liquid into measuring cup; skim fat and reserve 1 tablespoon (15 mL). Heat grapes in reserved fat just until hot. Arrange grapes over and around Cornish hens using slotted spoons.

5. Rinse cooker with remaining port, stirring to remove brown bits; pour into medium skillet. Add skimmed cooking liquid and the cream. Heat, stirring constantly, until smooth and bubbly. Pour over hens.

Lemon Chicken

Makes 4 servings

1	lemon
1	frying chicken (3 to 3 1/4 pounds or 1350 to 1450 g), cut into quarters
2	tablespoons (30 mL) flour
1	teaspoon (5 mL) salt
1/4	teaspoon (1 mL) paprika
2	tablespoons (30 mL) orange marmalade
1/4	cup (60 mL) dry sherry

Crisp chicken with a lively lemon flavor may remind you of a Chinese dish, but all the ingredients are easy to obtain — and to put together.

1. Soak top and bottom of 3 1/4-quart (3.25 L) clay cooker in water about 15 minutes; drain.

2. Grate lemon rind; squeeze juice. Sprinkle chicken quarters on both sides with lemon juice; coat with mixture of flour, salt and paprika. Place skin sides up in cooker. Mix lemon rind, marmalade and sherry; drizzle over chicken.

3. Place covered cooker in cold oven. Set oven at 450°F (230°C). Bake until chicken is tender, about 1 hour. Remove cover; bake until chicken is crisp and brown, 8 to 10 minutes.

4. Spoon sauce over chicken.

Turkey Mole

¹/₂   **cup (125 mL) blanched almonds**
4   **tablespoons (60 mL) toasted sesame seeds***
2   **dried small red chiles**
¹/₄   **teaspoon (1 mL) anise seeds**
1   **teaspoon (5 mL) salt**
¹/₂   **teaspoon (2 mL) ground cinnamon**
¹/₂   **teaspoon (2 mL) ground coriander**
¹/₄   **teaspoon (1 mL) ground cloves**
5   **pounds (2250 g) turkey drumsticks, thighs and large wing joints**
2   **medium onions, chopped**
3   **cloves garlic, minced**
1   **can (1 pound or 450 g) tomatoes, coarsley chopped, liquid reserved**
1   **cup (250 mL) regular-strength chicken broth, canned or homemade**
¹/₄   **cup (60 mL) tomato paste**
1   **square (1 ounce or 30 g) unsweetened chocolate, chopped**

The best known Mexican mole *is identified by an unexpected ingredient —* chocolate. *But really nothing about this subtly spiced, gently* piccante entré *is predictable. Somehow a dazzling assortment of spices and seeds comes together with amazing harmony. The turkey (use all dark meat, if possible) is served boneless, so you can spoon the mole over rice or roll it up in warm corn or flour tortillas to be eaten with the fingers.*

1. Soak top and bottom of 4³/₄-quart (4.75 L) clay cooker in water about 15 minutes; drain.

2. Process almonds, 3 tablespoons (45 mL) of the sesame seeds, the chiles and anise seeds in blender or food processor until powdery. Mix with salt, cinnamon, coriander and cloves.

3. Place turkey pieces in cooker, sprinkling layers with almond mixture. Combine onions, garlic, tomatoes with liquid, broth and tomato paste; pour into cooker.

4. Place covered cooker in cold oven. Set oven at 425°F (220°C). Bake, stirring once or twice, until turkey is brown and very tender, 2¹/₂ to 3 hours.

5. Remove turkey pieces from cooker. Process sauce, 2 cups (500 mL) at a time, in a blender or food processor until smooth. Transfer to bowl. Stir in chocolate until melted.

6. Remove and discard turkey bones. Return turkey meat in large pieces to cooker. Pour in sauce. Bake covered until very hot, 20 to 25 minutes. Sprinkle with remaining sesame seeds.

NOTE: *To toast sesame seeds, spread in shallow pan and bake in 350°F (180°C) oven, stirring occasionally, until brown, about 10 minutes.

Roast Turkey with Oyster Dressing

       Oyster Dressing (recipe follows)
1   **medium turkey (about 12 pounds or 5.5 kg), liver reserved for Oyster Dressing**
       Chicken broth, dry white wine or water
¹/₃   **cup (80 mL) all-purpose flour**
       Salt

If your clay cooker is large enough, you can indeed use it to roast a turkey for a family feast. What's more, the turkey will be exceptionally moist and flavorful. If you wish, use the giblets to make a rich broth for the gravy. Tangy Oyster Dressing makes a wonderful counterpoint to the turkey.

1. Soak top and bottom of 4³/₄-quart (4.75 L) clay cooker in water about 15 minutes; drain.

2. Make Oyster Dressing.

ROAST TURKEY WITH OYSTER DRESSING, continued

3. Rinse turkey and pat dry. Fill breast and body cavities with dressing; close openings with skewers or thread. Place turkey, breast side up, in cooker. Insert meat thermometer in thickest part of thigh.

4. Place covered cooker in cold oven. Set oven at 425°F (220°C). Bake until leg moves easily and thermometer registers 175°F (80°C), about 3 hours. (If juices begin to bubble over, remove with baster and reserve.)

5. Loosen skin that sticks to cooker and transfer turkey to board or platter. Pour cooking liquid into large measuring cup, scraping brown bits from side of cooker into liquid. Return turkey to cooker. Bake uncovered until dark brown, about 15 minutes.

6. Skim and reserve fat from cooking liquid. Add broth to cooking liquid to measure 3 cups (750 mL). Heat 1/3 cup (80 mL) of the reserved fat in large, deep skillet. Stir in flour; cook, stirring constantly, until bubbly and brown. Remove from heat; stir in 3 cups (750 mL) cooking liquid gradually. Cook, stirring constantly, until thickened. Simmer uncovered 5 minutes. Add salt, if needed.

7. Carve turkey; serve with dressing and gravy.

Makes about 8 cups (2 L)   ## *Oyster Dressing*

	Reserved turkey liver, chopped
2	medium onions, finely chopped
2	ribs celery, finely chopped
1/2	cup (125 mL) butter or margarine
7	cups (1750 mL) cubed day-old French bread
1/3	cup (80 mL) minced fresh parsley
1	teaspoon (5 mL) poultry seasoning
1	teaspoon (5 mL) salt
1/8	teaspoon (0.5 mL) white pepper
1	jar (8 ounces or 225 g) small oysters, drained, coarsely chopped
1/4 to 1/3	cup (60 to 80 mL) regular-strength chicken broth, homemade or canned

1. Sauté turkey liver, onions and celery in butter in large skillet until vegetables are soft but not brown.

2. Combine bread, parsley, poultry seasoning, salt and pepper in large bowl; stir in sautéed vegetables and the oysters; stir in both gradually. Mix gently just until moistened.

Marinated Chicken with Kumquats

Makes 6 servings

3   pounds (1350 g) meaty chicken
        pieces
1/3   cup (80 mL) dry white wine
2   tablespoons (30 mL) lime or
        lemon juice
2   tablespoons (30 mL) soy sauce
1   small onion, finely chopped
2   cloves garlic, minced
1/4   teaspoon (1 mL) dried oregano
        leaves
1/2   teaspoon (2 mL) curry powder
1/2   teaspoon (2 mL) ground ginger
1/2   cup (125 mL) sliced preserved
        kumquats, seeded
1   teaspoon (5 mL) cornstarch
1   tablespoon (15 mL) water

Polynesian flavors distinguish this chicken dish, sparkling with golden kumquat slices in a piquant sauce. The nutlike flavor of brown rice makes it a good choice for an accompaniment.

1. Place chicken pieces in shallow bowl. Combine wine, lime juice, soy sauce, onion, garlic, oregano, curry powder and ginger; pour over chicken. Refrigerate covered, turning once or twice, 8 hours or overnight.

2. Soak top and bottom of 3 1/4-quart (3.25 L) clay cooker in water about 15 minutes; drain.

3. Place chicken and marinade in cooker.

4. Place covered cooker in cold oven. Set oven at 450°F (230°C). Bake, stirring once or twice, until chicken is tender and brown, about 1 1/4 hours.

5. Pour off cooking liquid; skim and discard fat. Sprinkle chicken with kumquats. Turn off oven. Cover cooker and return to oven. Transfer liquid to a medium skillet. Mix cornstarch and water; stir into cooking liquid. Heat to boiling; cook, stirring constantly, until thickened and clear. Pour sauce over chicken and kumquats.

Chicken Breasts in Cream, Normandy

Makes 4 to 6 servings

1/2   pound (225 g) mushrooms,
        thinly sliced
2   shallots, finely chopped, or 2
        tablespoons (30 mL) finely
        chopped mild onion
1   tablespoon (15 mL) lemon
        juice
3   whole chicken breasts (about 3
        pounds or 1350 g), boned,
        skinned, cut into halves
1/4   cup (60 mL) Calvados or other
        brandy
3/4   teaspoon (4 mL) salt
1/8   teaspoon (0.5 mL) white
        pepper
3/4   cup (180 mL) whipping cream

The Norman touch in this simple yet attention-getting entrée is a fiery apple brandy called Calvados. If you must substitute, use applejack or other brandy.

1. Soak top and bottom of 2- to 3 1/4-quart (2 to 3.25 L) clay cooker in water about 15 minutes; drain.

2. Place mushrooms and shallots in cooker; sprinkle with lemon juice. Arrange chicken breasts, smooth sides up, in single layer over mushrooms. Pour in brandy. Sprinkle with salt and pepper. Pour in 1/2 cup (125 mL) of the cream.

3. Place covered cooker in cold oven. Set oven at 400°F (200°C). Bake until chicken breasts are tender, about 1 hour. Remove chicken breasts to warm serving bowl; keep warm.

4. Pour cooking liquid and mushrooms into medium skillet. Stir in remaining 1/4 cup (60 mL) cream. Heat to boiling; cook, stirring occasionally, until slightly thickened, 3 to 5 minutes. Pour sauce over chicken breasts.

Chicken Breasts with Walnuts

Makes 4 to 6 servings

3   whole chicken breasts (about 3 pounds or 1350 g), boned, skinned, cut into halves
3/4 teaspoon (4 mL) salt
    Pinch white pepper
1/4 pound (115 g) mushrooms, cut into quarters
1   shallot, finely chopped, or 1 tablespoon (15 mL) finely chopped, mild onion
2   cloves garlic, minced
2   teaspoons (10 mL) lemon juice
1   teaspoon (5 mL) Dijon-style mustard
1/3 cup (80 mL) dry white wine
1/4 teaspoon (1 mL) crumbled dried tarragon leaves
1/3 cup (80 mL) coarsely chopped toasted walnuts*
1/2 cup (125 mL) whipping cream

Oven-simmered in a clay cooker, chicken breasts remain moist and juicy, a lovely foil for toasted walnuts and a well seasoned cream sauce. Good accompaniments are fluffy rice and steamed asparagus spears.

1. Soak top and bottom of 2- to 3 1/4-quart (2 to 3.25 L) clay cooker in water about 15 minutes; drain.

2. Sprinkle chicken breasts on both sides with salt and pepper; place in cooker. Sprinkle with mushrooms, shallot and garlic. Mix lemon juice and mustard; stir in wine. Pour over chicken. Sprinkle with tarragon.

3. Place covered cooker in cold oven. Set oven at 400°F (200°C). Bake, stirring gently once, until chicken breasts are tender and light brown, 50 minutes to 1 hour. Pour cooking liquid into medium skillet. Sprinkle chicken with walnuts; cover cooker to keep chicken warm.

4. Add cream to cooking liquid. Heat to boiling; cook, stirring occasionally, until sauce is slightly thickened; pour over chicken and walnuts.

NOTE: *To toast walnuts, spread in shallow pan and bake in oven with chicken until brown, 6 to 8 minutes.

Chicken with Forty Cloves of Garlic

Makes 5 to 6 servings

1   tablespoon (15 mL) olive oil
40 cloves garlic, whole, peeled
1/4 teaspoon (1 mL) dried rosemary leaves, crumbled
1/4 teaspoon (1 mL) dried thyme leaves
1/8 teaspoon (0.5 mL) crumbled sage leaves
1   whole large frying chicken (4 to 4 1/2 pounds or 1800 g to 2 kg)
1   tablespoon (15 mL) lemon juice
    Salt
    Pepper
    Sliced French bread

Formidable as it sounds, this astonishing quantity of garlic (about a bulb and a half) actually cooks to a gently sweet flavor with roast chicken in clay. Try it as it is served in Provence — spreading the soft garlic on crusty French bread.

1. Soak top and bottom of 3 1/4-quart (3.25 L) clay cooker in water about 15 minutes; drain. Line bottom and sides of cooker with parchment paper.

2. Combine olive oil, garlic and herbs in cooker. Rinse chicken and pat dry reserving neck and giblets for other use. Place chicken over garlic mixture. Drizzle with lemon juice. Sprinkle with salt and pepper.

3. Place covered cooker in cold oven. Set oven at 475°F (250°C). Bake until chicken is tender and juices run clear when thigh is pierced, about 1 1/4 hours. Remove cover; bake until chicken is crisp and brown, 5 to 10 minutes.

4. Carve chicken and spoon cooking liquid over chicken. Serve with garlic and French bread.

Makes 4 to 5 servings

Gingered Roast Chicken with Nectarines

1   **whole frying chicken (about 3¹/₂ pounds or 1600 g)**
2   **large nectarines (about 12 ounces or 340 g), unpared, cut into wedges, pitted**
2   **tablespoons (30 mL) brown sugar**
¹/₂   **teaspoon (2 mL) ground ginger**
¹/₄   **teaspoon (1 mL) ground nutmeg**
2   **tablespoons (30 mL) butter or margarine**

Preparing this enticing combination of chicken and spiced fruit is simplicity itself. In the clay cooker all the flavors mingle to become something new and wonderful. Brown or white rice makes a nice foil for the chicken and nectarine juices, along with a green vegetable and a fruity white wine, such as a California Chenin Blanc.

1. Soak top and bottom of 2-quart (2 L) clay cooker in water about 15 minutes; drain.

2. Rinse chicken and pat dry, reserving neck and giblets for other use. Place chicken, breast side up, in cooker. Surround with nectarines. Mix brown sugar, ginger and nutmeg; sprinkle over chicken and fruit. Dot chicken and fruit with butter.

3. Place covered cooker in cold oven. Set oven at 475°F (250°C). Bake 1 hour. Remove cover; bake until chicken is crisp and brown, 5 to 10 minutes.

4. Carve chicken; spoon fruit and cooking juices over chicken.

Makes 4 servings

Chicken with Almonds and Apples

1   **small onion, finely chopped**
1   **rib celery, finely chopped**
1   **medium carrot, pared, shredded**
¹/₄   **cup (60 mL) brandy**
1   **frying chicken (3 to 3¹/₂ pounds or 1350 to 1600 g), cut into quarters**
¹/₂   **cup (125 mL) dry white wine**
1   **teaspoon (5 mL) salt**
   Pinch white pepper
¹/₈   **teaspoon (0.5 mL) ground nutmeg**
2   **medium tart cooking apples, pared, cored, cut into wedges**
2   **tablespoons (30 mL) sliced almonds**
1   **tablespoon (15 mL) butter or margarine**
¹/₂   **cup (125 mL) whipping cream**

Apples cook with chicken quarters and a gentle mixture of vegetables to produce an agreeable sweet-savory blend of flavors in an almond-topped cream sauce.

1. Soak top and bottom of 3¹/₄-quart (3.25 L) clay cooker in water about 15 minutes; drain.

2. Combine onion, celery and carrot in cooker; pour in brandy. Place chicken quarters, skin sides up, over vegetables; pour in wine. Sprinkle chicken with salt, pepper and nutmeg.

3. Place covered cooker in cold oven. Set oven at 450°F (230°C). Bake 45 minutes. Place apple wedges around chicken. Bake covered until chicken is tender and brown, about 30 minutes. Remove chicken and apples to warm serving bowl; keep warm.

4. Sauté almonds in butter, until light brown.

5. Pour cooking liquid with vegetables into medium skillet. Stir in cream. Heat to boiling; cook, stirring occasionally, until slightly thickened, 3 to 5 minutes. Pour sauce over chicken and apples. Sprinkle with almonds.

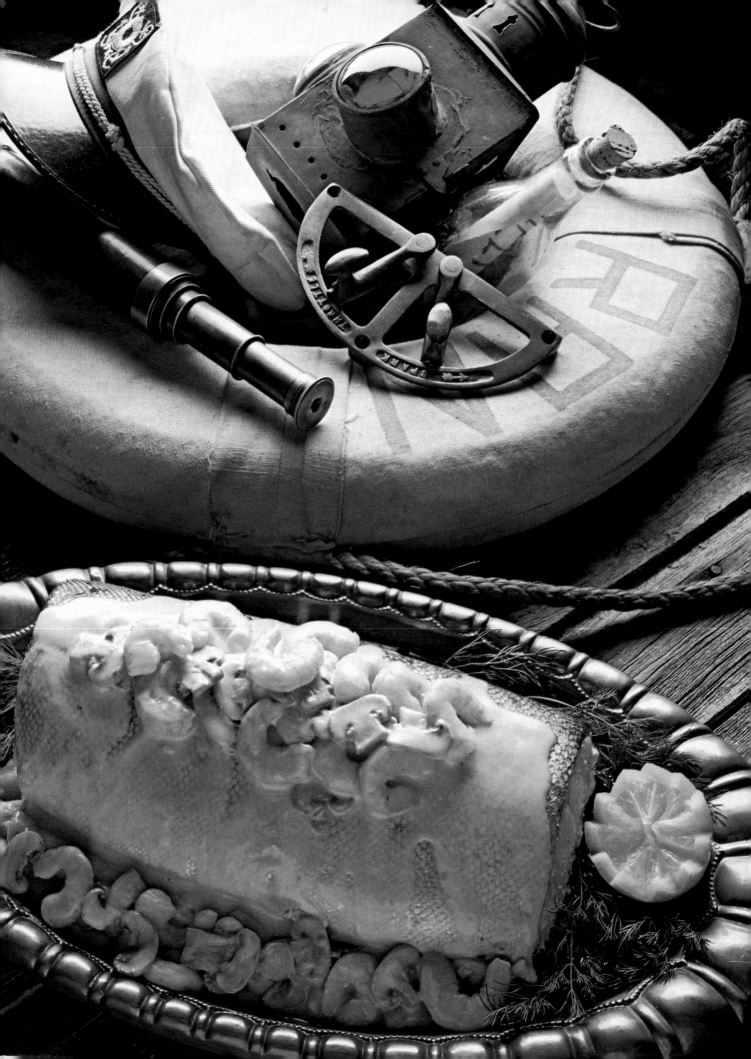

Tender, Moist Seafood

Even accomplished cooks admit that cooking fish well can be tricky. In that sense, a clay cooker can perform almost magically to prepare fish and shellfish superbly.

Two important factors in cooking seafood skillfully are time and temperature. Cooked too long or with too much heat, fish can be dry and seem tough. Seafood is really quite fragile and requires special care in the kitchen. A clay cooker fulfills these demands—providing a steady temperature and surrounding fish or shellfish with the moisture of steam. And as with other foods, the flavor can't be excelled.

When you bake fish in an unglazed clay cooker, it is a good idea to line it with baking parchment paper to prevent fishy flavor from carrying over into later dishes. However, clay cooking so suits fish that, if you serve it often, you may wish to keep one clay cooker just for fish. A long slender clay cooker designed especially for fish is available; its capacity is approximately 2¾ quarts (2.75 L). It is particularly well suited for poaching whole fish.

The unpleasant flavor many people associate with fishiness is actually the taste of old fish. When purchasing fish or shellfish, shop around until you find a fish dealer whose wares are strictly fresh. Don't buy fish that has a strong odor. Other signs of freshness to look for are firmness and clear, natural color. Avoid cut fish that looks brown, murky or dry at the edges. After you bring fish home, refrigerate it immediately, then cook it within two days.

For both experienced and new cooks, the happiest surprise about using a clay cooker for fish is that even elaborate dishes are so easy. Fish can be oven-poached in a clay cooker in a very simple flavored liquid. When you want to make a sauce, tilt the cover of the clay cooker just enough to pour out the cooking liquid; thicken the liquid or add cream to complete the sauce. The fish stays warm in the covered clay pot while you prepare the sauce.

No matter what style of cooking or what variety of fish and shellfish you choose, you will be happy with the results when you make it in a clay cooker.

Makes 8 to 10 servings

Oven-Poached Salmon with Shrimp Sauce

1   **piece whole salmon (4 to 5 pounds or 1800 to 2250 g, without head or tail)**
    Salt
    White pepper
¹/₂   **pound (225 g) raw small shrimp, shelled, deveined**
1   **lemon, thinly sliced**
1   **small onion, thinly sliced**
3   **sprigs parsley**
¹/₂   **cup (125 mL) dry white wine**
¹/₄   **cup (60 mL) water**
¹/₄   **pound (115 g) fresh mushrooms, thinly sliced**
3   **tablespoons (45 mL) butter or margarine**
1¹/₂   **tablespoons (22 mL) flour**
1   **egg yolk**
¹/₂   **cup (125 mL) sour cream**
    Minced fresh parsley

Lining the clay cooker with baking parchment paper for this recipe gives you a handy way of transferring the rather bulky salmon neatly intact to a serving platter. This elegant salmon and shrimp entrée, with creamy mushroom sauce, is especially appropriate for entertaining. Serve with rice and fresh green beans, accompanied by a dry white wine, such as a California Sauvignon Blanc or Fumé Blanc. You can use this same basic oven poaching method (omitting shrimp) for other large whole fish, served warm or chilled.

1. Soak top and bottom of long 2³/₄-quart (2.75 L) clay cooker in water about 15 minutes; drain. Line bottom and sides of cooker with parchment paper.

2. Wipe salmon with damp paper toweling. Sprinkle inside and out lightly with salt and pepper. Place in cooker. Top with shrimp, lemon, onion and parsley sprigs; pour in wine and water.

3. Place covered cooker in cold oven. Set oven at 450°F (230°C). Bake until shrimp are pink and salmon easily flakes with fork, about 45 minutes.

4. About 5 minutes before salmon is done, sauté mushrooms in butter in 1¹/₂-quart (1.5 L) saucepan until light brown.

5. Remove and discard lemon and onion slices and parsley from cooker. Pour off cooking liquid, reserving 1 cup (250 mL). Cover cooker to keep salmon and shrimp warm.

6. Stir flour into mushrooms to make smooth paste; cook until bubbly. Remove from heat; stir in reserved cooking liquid gradually. Heat to boiling; cook, stirring constantly, until sauce is thick, 3 to 5 minutes.

7. Beat egg yolk and sour cream in small bowl. Stir in a little of the hot sauce until smooth. Stir egg mixture into hot sauce; cook over low heat, stirring constantly until thickened (do not boil).

8. Transfer salmon and shrimp to a warm serving platter. Cover with mushroom sauce. Garnish with minced parsley.

Makes 4 servings

Creamy Baked Scallops

1¹/₂   **pounds (675 g) scallops**
³/₄   **teaspoon (4 mL) salt**
¹/₈   **teaspoon (0.5 mL) white pepper**
    Pinch cayenne pepper
    Pinch ground nutmeg

Steamed new potatoes and broccoli spears will complement these sea scallops served in a tart, lemon cream sauce.

1. Soak top and bottom of 2- to 3¹/₄-quart (2 to 3.25 L) clay cooker in water about 15 minutes; drain. Line bottom and sides of cooker with parchment paper.

CREAMY BAKED SCALLOPS, continued

1 bay leaf
1 shallot, finely chopped, or 1
    tablespoon (15 mL) finely
    chopped mild onion
2 tablespoons (30 mL) minced
    fresh parsley
2 tablespoons (30 mL) butter or
    margarine
1/4 cup (60 mL) dry white wine
2 tablespoons (30 mL) lemon
    juice
2 teaspoons (10 mL) cornstarch
1 tablespoon (15 mL) water
1/2 cup (125 mL) whipping cream
1 egg yolk
1/4 cup (60 mL) shredded
    Monterey Jack cheese
    Minced fresh parsley

2. Sprinkle scallops with salt, white and cayenne peppers and nutmeg. Place in cooker. Insert bay leaf near center; sprinkle with shallot and 2 tablespoons (30 mL) parsley. Melt butter; stir in wine and lemon juice. Pour butter mixture over scallops.

3. Place covered cooker in cold oven. Set oven at 450°F (230°C). Bake, stirring once, until scallops are firm and white, 25 to 30 minutes.

4. Remove scallops with slotted spoon to warm serving dish; keep warm. Pour cooking liquid into medium saucepan; discard bay leaf. Mix cornstarch and water; add cornstarch mixture and cream to saucepan. Cook, stirring constantly, over high heat until bubbly. Beat egg yolk in small bowl; stir in a little of the hot sauce. Stir egg yolk mixture into sauce; stir in cheese. Cook, stirring constantly, over low heat, 2 minutes (do not boil).

5. Pour sauce over scallops. Garnish with parsley.

Shrimp Jambalaya

Makes 4 to 6 servings

1 cup (250 mL) uncooked long-
    grain white rice
1 large onion, finely chopped
1 clove garlic, minced
1 cup (250 mL) julienne-cut ham
    strips
1/4 cup (60 mL) minced fresh
    parsley
1 teaspoon (5 mL) salt
1/2 teaspoon (2 mL) chili powder
1/4 teaspoon (1 mL) dried thyme
    leaves
1/8 teaspoon (0.5 mL) cayenne
    pepper
1 can (1 pound or 450 g)
    tomatoes, coarsely chopped,
    liquid reserved
1 can (14 1/2 ounces or 415 g)
    regular-strength chicken
    broth
1 can (8 ounces or 225 g) tomato
    sauce
1 bay leaf
1 pound (450 g) raw shrimp,
    shelled, deveined
    Minced fresh parsley

A fine meal-in-one, this Creole dish needs only some crisp vegetable relishes and a loaf of crusty bread to make a satisfying repast.

1. Soak top and bottom of 3 1/4-quart (3.25 L) clay cooker in water about 15 minutes; drain.

2. Combine rice, onion, garlic, ham, 1/4 cup (60 mL) parsley, the salt, chili powder, thyme and cayenne in cooker. Stir in tomatoes, broth and tomato sauce; insert bay leaf near center.

3. Place covered cooker in cold oven. Set oven at 450°F (230°C). Bake, stirring after 45 minutes, just until rice is tender, about 1 hour. Arrange shrimp in single layer over rice. Bake covered until shrimp are firm and pink, about 10 minutes.

4. Serve in shallow soup bowls or individual casseroles; garnish with parsley.

Makes 4 to 6 servings

Sole Fillets with Tomato Cream Sauce

3	medium tomatoes, peeled, seeded, chopped
1	shallot, finely chopped, or 1 tablespoon (15 mL) finely chopped mild onion
1	tablespoon (15 mL) minced fresh parsley
1	small clove garlic, minced
1/8	teaspoon (0.5 mL) dried thyme leaves
1/4	bay leaf
2	pounds (900 g) sole fillets
	Salt
	White pepper
2	tablespoons (30 mL) butter or margarine
1/4	cup (60 mL) dry white wine
1/2	cup (125 mL) whipping cream
	Minced fresh parsley

Here is a classic and beautiful treatment of sole (Sole Duglére). *It is similar to* Sole Bonne Femme, *with chopped fresh tomatoes in place of mushrooms. Serve the fish and sauce with rice.*

1. Soak top and bottom of 3 1/4-quart (3.25 L) clay cooker in water about 15 minutes; drain. Line bottom and sides of cooker with parchment paper.

2. Spread chopped tomatoes in cooker. Sprinkle with shallots, 1 tablespoon (15 mL) parsley, the garlic and thyme; insert bay leaf near center. Wipe fillets with damp paper toweling; sprinkle both sides lightly with salt and pepper. Fold fillets in half and arrange, slightly overlapping, in cooker. Dot with butter. Pour in wine.

3. Place covered cooker in cold oven. Set oven at 450°F (230°C). Bake until fish barely flakes with fork, about 30 minutes.

4. Remove fish carefully with slotted spatula to warm platter, keep warm. Pour tomatoes and cooking liquid into large skillet. Discard bay leaf. Stir in cream. Heat to boiling; cook, stirring until slightly thickened. Pour sauce over fish. Garnish with minced parsley.

Makes 2 servings

Curried Salmon Steaks with New Potatoes

2	salmon steaks (each about 8 ounces or 225 g), 1 inch (2.5 cm) thick
1	tablespoon (15 mL) flour
1/2	teaspoon (2 mL) salt
1/2	teaspoon (2 mL) curry powder
1/4	teaspoon (1 mL) paprika
3	small new potatoes, unpared, cut into 1/4-inch (0.5 cm) slices
2	tablespoons (30 mL) butter or margarine, melted
1	tablespoon (15 mL) lemon juice
2	teaspoons (10 mL) mustard seeds, coarsely crushed
	Thinly sliced green onions
	Chutney, if desired

Salmon makes a distinctive dinner for two from the clay cooker, seasoned with curry powder and mustard seeds and baked with sliced new potatoes. Add a green vegetable to complete the menu.

1. Soak top and bottom of 3 1/4-quart (3.25 L) clay cooker in water about 15 minutes; drain. Line bottom and sides of cooker with parchment paper.

2. Wipe salmon steaks with damp paper toweling. Coat with a mixture of flour, salt, curry powder and paprika. Place in cooker. Arrange potatoes, standing on edge, around salmon. Mix butter, lemon juice and mustard seeds; drizzle over salmon and potatoes.

3. Place covered cooker in cold oven. Set oven at 450°F (230°C). Bake until salmon is firm and potatoes are tender, about 35 minutes. Remove cover; bake until salmon is brown, about 10 minutes.

4. Drizzle salmon and potatoes with cooking liquid; sprinkle with green onions. Serve with chutney.

Chinese Steamed Fish with Black Beans

Makes 6 servings

2   tablespoons (30 mL) fermented black beans*
1   large clove garlic, minced
3   thin slices pared fresh ginger root, finely chopped, or ¼ teaspoon (1 mL) ground ginger
¼   cup (60 mL) soy sauce
1   tablespoon (15 mL) vegetable oil
1   teaspoon (5 mL) sugar
2   pounds (900 g) halibut or sea bass steaks or fillets
1   green onion with top, thinly sliced

The moist air inside a clay cooker makes it possible to use it as an oven steamer for this flavorful Chinese dish. Make it with firm-fleshed fish low in fat, such as halibut or sea bass. If you are selecting several dishes for a Chinese meal, this is one that can cook unattended in the oven as you stir-fry another on top of the range.

1. Soak top and bottom of 3¼-quart (3.25 L) clay cooker in water about 15 minutes; drain. Line bottom and sides of cooker with parchment paper.

2. Rinse and drain black beans; crush in small bowl with fork. Stir in garlic and ginger root to make paste. Stir in soy sauce, oil and sugar. Wipe fish with damp paper toweling. Place fish in single layer in cooker. Spoon bean mixture over fish.

3. Place covered cooker in cold oven. Set oven at 450°F (230°C). Bake until fish easily flakes with fork, about 30 minutes.

4. Remove fish carefully with a slotted spatula to warm serving platter; spoon on some of the cooking liquid. Sprinkle with green onion.

NOTE: *Fermented black beans are available in Oriental markets. There is no substitute.

Cioppino

Makes 6 servings

1   large onion, finely chopped
1   green pepper, chopped
2   cloves garlic, minced
⅓   cup (80 mL) minced fresh parsley
1   can (15 ounces or 425 g) tomato purée
1   can (8 ounces or 225 g) tomato sauce
1   cup (250 mL) water
1   cup (250 mL) dry red wine
2   teaspoons (10 mL) salt
⅛   teaspoon (0.5 mL) white pepper
¼   teaspoon (1 mL) dried thyme leaves
⅛   teaspoon (0.5 mL) dried rosemary leaves

This mixed seafood stew is generally credited to the Italian seamen who worked from San Francisco's Fisherman's Wharf in its heyday. It is best made with meaty Dungeness crab from the Pacific. The crab is cut up (detaching the claws and cutting the body into several pieces), then cracked with a mallot. Eat the crab with your fingers. Provide bibs when you serve this dish, as you would with lobster. Use the pointed tip of one of the claws to dig out the meat. Nutcrackers at the table come in handy if additional cracking is needed.

 Accompany Cioppino with hot, buttery garlic bread and a green salad. A light red wine, such as a Grignolino or Barbera, accompanies this assertively seasoned dish well.

1. Soak top and bottom of 4¾-quart (4.75 L) clay cooker in water about 15 minutes; drain. Line bottom and sides of cooker with parchment paper.

2. Combine onion, green pepper, garlic, parsley, tomato purée, tomato sauce, water, wine, salt, pepper, thyme and rosemary in cooker.

CIOPPINO, continued

2	medium Dungeness crabs, (each about 1¹/₂ pounds or 675 g), cooked, cleaned, cracked
2	rock cod fillets (about ³/₄ pound or 340 g), cut into 1¹/₂-inch (4 cm) pieces
1	pound (450 g) raw shrimp, shelled, deveined
1	dozen fresh clams in shells, scrubbed

3. Place covered cooker in cold oven. Set oven at 425°F (220°C). Bake, stirring once or twice, until sauce is thick, about 1 hour.

4. Stir in crab, fish fillets, shrimp and clams. Bake covered until crab is hot, shrimp are pink and clam shells open (discard any clams that do not open), about 45 minutes.

5. Serve seafood in large soup bowls; spoon sauce over seafood.

Makes 4 to 6 servings

Red Snapper Veracruz

2	medium onions, thinly sliced, separated into rings
1	green pepper, cut into thin strips
2	cloves garlic, minced
1	can (1 pound or 450 g) tomatoes, coarsely chopped, liquid reserved
¹/₄	cup (60 mL) sliced pimiento-stuffed olives
1	tablespoon (15 mL) drained capers
2	tablespoons (30 mL) tomato paste
2	tablespoons (30 mL) chopped fresh or 2 teaspoons (10 mL) dried coriander leaves (Chinese parsley), if desired
2	teaspoons (10 mL) grated orange rind
1	teaspoon (5 mL) salt
¹/₂	teaspoon (2 mL) dried oregano leaves
¹/₂	teaspoon (2 mL) ground cumin
1	bay leaf
1	dried small red chile, crushed
2	pounds (900 g) red snapper fillets
	Salt
	Pepper
	Coriander sprigs, if desired

Make the festive Mexican-style sauce with tomatoes, olives, orange and a snappy dried chile in the clay cooker first. Then poach fish fillets in the sauce, about 20 minutes; serve with rice and well-chilled dark beer.

1. Soak top and bottom of 3¹/₄-quart (3.25 L) clay cooker in water about 15 minutes; drain. Line bottom and sides of cooker with parchment paper.

2. Combine onions, green pepper, garlic, tomatoes, olives, capers, tomato paste, 2 tablespoons (30 mL) coriander, the orange rind, 1 teaspoon (5 mL) salt, the oregano, cumin, bay leaf and dried chile; add to cooker.

3. Place covered cooker in cold oven. Set oven at 450°F (230°C). Bake stirring once or twice, until sauce is flavorful and thick, about 2 hours.

4. Wipe fillets with damp paper toweling. Sprinkle both sides lightly with salt and pepper. Remove and reserve about half the sauce from cooker; discard bay leaf. Place fish fillets, slightly overlapping, in remaining sauce in cooker. Cover with reserved sauce.

5. Bake covered until fish is white and firm, about 20 minutes. Garnish with coriander sprigs.

Makes 4 servings

Herb-Stuffed Trout

1	small onion, finely chopped
5	tablespoons (75 mL) butter or margarine
1	clove garlic, minced
1	cup (250 mL) fresh bread crumbs
1/4	cup (60 mL) minced fresh parsley
1	teaspoon (5 mL) fines herbes
2	tablespoons (30 mL) lemon juice
4	whole trout (each about 8 ounces or 225 g)
	Salt
	Pepper
1 1/2	tablespoons (22 mL) flour
1/4	teaspoon (1 mL) paprika
	Parsley sprigs
	Lemon wedges

Trout is always a treat for fish lovers, and never more so than when baked with a lemon and herb-flavored stuffing.

1. Soak top and bottom of 3 1/4-quart (3.25 L) clay cooker in water about 15 minutes; drain. Line bottom and sides of cooker with parchment paper.

2. Sauté onion in 4 tablespoons (60 mL) of the butter in medium skillet until soft and light brown; stir in garlic. Remove from heat. Stir in bread crumbs, 1/4 cup (60 mL) parsley, the fines herbes and 1 tablespoon (15 mL) of the lemon juice.

3. Wipe trout with damp paper toweling. Sprinkle inside and out with salt and pepper. Brush with remaining 1 tablespoon (15 mL) lemon juice. Coat with mixture of flour and paprika. Fill cavities with bread crumb mixture.

4. Place trout, side by side, in cooker. Melt remaining butter; drizzle over fish.

5. Place covered cooker in cold oven. Set oven at 450°F (230°C). Bake until trout are firm and opaque, about 35 minutes. Remove cover; bake until brown, 10 to 15 minutes.

6. Garnish trout with parsley sprigs and lemon wedges.

Makes 4 to 6 servings

Dilled Fillets of Sole

2	pounds (900 g) sole fillets
	Salt
	Freshly ground pepper
1/4	cup (60 mL) butter or margarine, melted
1 1/2	tablespoons (22 mL) minced fresh parsley
1	shallot, finely chopped, or 1 tablespoon (15 mL) finely chopped mild onion
1/2	teaspoon (2 mL) dried dill weed
1	tablespoon (15 mL) lemon juice

Accompanied by tiny, whole new potatoes, buttery dill-flecked sole has a Scandinavian accent.

1. Soak top and bottom of 3 1/4-quart (3.25 L) clay cooker in water about 15 minutes; drain. Line bottom and sides of cooker with parchment paper.

2. Wipe fillets with damp paper toweling; sprinkle both sides lightly with salt and pepper. Combine butter, parsley, shallot and dill weed. Drizzle some of the butter mixture over fish. Fold fillets in half and arrange, slightly overlapping, in cooker. Drizzle with remaining butter mixture.

3. Place covered cooker in cold oven. Set oven at 450°F (230°C). Bake until fish barely flakes with fork, 25 to 30 minutes.

4. Remove fish carefully with slotted spatula to warm platter. Spoon some of the cooking liquid over fish. Sprinkle with lemon juice.

Crab Soufflé

5	tablespoons (75 mL) butter or margarine
1/4	cup (60 mL) all-purpose flour
1/2	teaspoon (2 mL) salt
1/4	teaspoon (1 mL) dry mustard
1/8	teaspoon (0.5 mL) cayenne pepper
1 1/2	cups (375 mL) milk
2	cups (500 mL) shredded Swiss cheese
6	eggs, separated
1/2	pound (225 g) flaked cooked crabmeat
1	rib celery, finely chopped
2	green onions with tops, thinly sliced
1	tablespoon (15 mL) lemon juice
1/8	teaspoon (0.5 mL) cream of tartar

A clay cooker produces an appealingly crusty soufflé, as this recipe for a brunch or light supper main dish demonstrates.

1. Soak top and bottom of 3 1/4-quart (3.25 L) clay cooker in water about 15 minutes; drain.

2. Melt 4 tablespoons (60 mL) of the butter in medium saucepan; stir in flour, salt, mustard and cayenne. Cook until bubbly; remove from heat. Stir in milk gradually. Cook, stirring constantly, until thickened and smooth. Stir in cheese; cook until melted. Remove from heat.

3. Beat egg yolks, one at a time, into sauce. Stir in crab, celery, green onions and lemon juice.

4. Melt remaining butter; pat dry and brush sides and bottom of cooker with butter. Beat egg whites with cream of tartar until stiff but not dry. Fold gently into crabmeat mixture. Pour into cooker.

5. Place covered cooker gently in cold oven. Set oven at 400°F (200°C). Bake until soufflé is puffed and brown, about 1 hour. Serve immediately.

Shrimp de Jonghe

6	tablespoons (90 mL) butter or margarine
1	cup (250 mL) fresh bread crumbs
2	tablespoons (30 mL) grated Parmesan cheese
1/4	cup (60 mL) minced fresh parsley
1	clove garlic, minced
1/4	teaspoon (1 mL) salt
1/4	teaspoon (1 mL) paprika
1/4	teaspoon (1 mL) dried thyme leaves
1/8	teaspoon (0.5 mL) dried tarragon leaves
1	pound (450 g) large raw shrimp (20 to 25), shelled, deveined
2	tablespoons (30 mL) dry sherry wine

Sweetly tender shrimp with a delicate sherry and butter flavor make one more classic seafood dish that can be easily produced in a clay cooker. Accompany the shrimp with whole green beans, cherry tomatoes and a chilled Chablis.

1. Soak top and bottom of 2-quart (2 L) clay cooker in water about 15 minutes; drain. Line bottom and sides of cooker with parchment paper.

2. Melt butter in small saucepan; mix 2 tablespoons (30 mL) of the butter, the bread crumbs and cheese in bowl. Reserve bread crumb mixture.

3. Stir parsley, garlic, salt, paprika, thyme and tarragon into remaining butter. Place shrimp in cooker. Pour butter mixture over shrimp. Drizzle with sherry.

4. Place covered cooker in cold oven. Set oven at 450°F (230°C). Bake, stirring once, just until shrimp are pink, about 20 minutes. Sprinkle with bread crumb mixture; bake uncovered until topping browns, 10 to 12 minutes.

Swordfish Stroganoff

1   **medium onion, thinly sliced, separated into rings**
1/4 **pound (115 g) mushrooms, thinly sliced**
2   **tablespoons (30 mL) butter or margarine**
1 1/2 **pounds (675 g) swordfish steaks**
1 1/2 **tablespoons (22 mL) flour**
1/4 **teaspoon (1 mL) paprika**
1   **teaspoon (5 mL) salt**
     Pinch white pepper
1/4 **cup (60 mL) dry white wine**
2   **teaspoons (10 mL) lemon juice**
1   **teaspoon (5 mL) Dijon-style mustard**
1   **teaspoon (5 mL) Worcestershire sauce**
1   **cup (250 mL) sour cream**
     Minced fresh parsley
     Paprika

Swordfish is often said to have an almost meaty flavor. Appropriately, it makes a savory stroganoff to serve over green noodles. Accompany with a basket of cherry tomatoes and a light rye bread.

1. Soak top and bottom of 3 1/4-quart (3.25 L) clay cooker in water about 15 minutes; drain. Line bottom and sides of cooker with parchment paper.

2. Place onions and mushrooms in cooker; dot with butter.

3. Place covered cooker in cold oven. Set oven at 450°F (230°C). Bake, stirring once or twice, until onions are limp, about 30 minutes.

4. Wipe swordfish steaks with damp paper toweling. Cut into strips about 2 inches (5 cm) long by 1/2 inch (1.5 cm) wide. Combine flour, 1/4 teaspoon (1 mL) paprika, the salt and pepper; coat fish lightly with mixture. Add fish strips to cooker. Mix wine, lemon juice, mustard and Worcestershire sauce; pour into cooker.

5. Bake covered, stirring once, until fish is white and firm, about 20 minutes. Stir in sour cream. Turn off oven. Cover cooker and return to oven until sauce is hot, 5 to 10 minutes. Garnish with parsley and paprika.

Almond-Crusted Trout with Lemon Butter

5   **tablespoons (75 mL) butter or margarine, room temperature**
1   **shallot, finely chopped, or 1 tablespoon (15 mL) finely chopped mild onion**
1   **tablespoon (15 mL) minced fresh parsley**
1   **teaspoon (5 mL) grated lemon rind**
1/8 **teaspoon (0.5 mL) paprika**
1/2 **teaspoon (2 mL) salt**
     Pinch white pepper
2   **teaspoons (10 mL) lemon juice**
4   **whole trout (each about 8 ounces or 225 g)**
1/4 **cup (60 mL) sliced almonds**
     Watercress sprigs

This recipe makes the most of the affinity of trout for both almonds and lemon — the lemon butter tucked inside and the almonds crusting the surface.

1. Soak top and bottom of 3 1/4-quart (3.25 L) clay cooker in water about 15 minutes; drain. Line bottom and sides of cooker with parchment paper.

2. Place 4 tablespoons (60 mL) of the butter in small mixing bowl; cream until light and fluffy. Add shallot, parsley, lemon rind, paprika, salt and pepper; mix until blended. Beat in lemon juice gradually.

3. Wipe trout with damp paper toweling. Place a fourth of the lemon butter in cavity of each trout. Place trout, side by side, in cooker. Melt remaining butter; brush over fish. Sprinkle with almonds.

4. Place covered cooker in cold oven. Set oven at 450°F (230°C). Bake until trout are firm and opaque, about 35 minutes. Remove cover; bake until almonds brown, 10 to 15 minutes.

5. Spoon melted lemon butter over trout; garnish with watercress.

Vegetables and Side Dishes

As meat prices soar, many people are looking to vegetables as a more economical source of protein and other essential nutrients; and vegetable gardens flourish as never before.

To cook fresh produce superbly, whether it comes from the market or your own backyard, a clay cooker cannot be excelled. Use it for both vegetable accompaniments and main dishes.

Vegetables cooked in clay need very little added water. The steam from the soaked clay cooker keeps them moist at first, time enough for many vegetables to cook tender-crisp. Using water sparingly when cooking vegetables makes them more nutritious because certain vitamins dissolve in water and are often lost when vegetables are drained.

The other enemy of vegetables' vitamin content is heat. Too much for too long will destroy valuable components. When you cook vegetables in a clay cooker, check them for doneness a little before you expect them to complete cooking. Learn to enjoy the appealing crispness and true flavor of slightly undercooked vegetables from the versatile clay cooker.

You will be amazed at the variety of cooking styles possible for vegetables in a clay cooker—simple steaming with a light sauce, hearty baked casseroles, crumb-topped gratins and even light vegetable soufflés.

Baking times of the vegetable and side dish recipes in this chapter have been planned to coincide with the oven temperatures used for most meat and poultry main dishes. This offers you the opportunity to use your oven for two clay cookers at the same time.

For vegetable lovers, then, clay cookers can take you from A (as in asparagus) to Z (for zucchini).

Makes 3 to 4 servings

Asparagus with Almond Butter

1 pound (450 g) fresh asparagus, ends trimmed
1/8 teaspoon (0.5 mL) dried tarragon leaves
1/4 cup (60 mL) water
1/4 cup (60 mL) butter or margarine
1/4 cup (60 mL) dry white wine
1 teaspoon (5 mL) Dijon-style mustard
1 shallot, finely chopped, or 1 tablespoon (15 mL) finely chopped mild onion
1/4 cup (60 mL) sliced almonds
Salt

Delicious with sautéed fish, you can make the almond butter while the asparagus steams to tarragon-scented tenderness in a clay cooker.

1. Soak top and bottom of 2-quart (2 L) clay cooker in water about 15 minutes; drain.

2. Place asparagus in cooker. Sprinkle with tarragon; pour in water.

3. Place covered cooker in cold oven. Set oven at 425°F (220°C). Bake just until asparagus is tender, 15 to 20 minutes; drain.

4. While asparagus is cooking, heat butter, wine, mustard and shallot in small sauce pan. Boil, stirring constantly, until liquid is reduced by about half. Stir in almonds; cook just until almonds are light brown, 2 to 3 minutes. Pour almond butter over asparagus. Taste and add salt as needed.

Makes 6 servings

Onion and Almond Soufflé

1/4 cup (60 mL) butter or margarine
3 large onions, finely chopped
2 tablespoons (15 mL) flour
3/4 teaspoon (4 mL) salt
1/8 teaspoon (0.5 mL) white pepper
Pinch ground nutmeg
1/4 cup (60 mL) half-and-half
6 eggs, separated
1/8 teaspoon (0.5 mL) cream of tartar
2 tablespoons (30 mL) slivered almonds

A soufflé gives a lift to an otherwise ordinary meal. Try this sweet onion soufflé with roast chicken or lamb and a green vegetable.

1. Soak top and bottom of 2-quart (2 L) clay cooker in water about 15 minutes; drain.

2. Melt butter in large saucepan; remove and reserve 1 tablespoon (15 mL) of butter. Stir onions into remaining melted butter until well coated; cook covered over medium heat, stirring occasionally, until onions are limp and golden and most of the liquid has evaporated, about 20 minutes. Stir in flour, salt, pepper and nutmeg; remove from heat. Stir in half-and-half gradually. Return to heat and cook, stirring constantly, until thick. Stir in egg yolks; remove from heat.

3. Beat egg whites and cream of tartar until peaks are short and distinct when beaters are raised. Fold beaten egg whites gently into onion mixture.

4. Pat dry and brush sides and bottom of cooker with reserved butter. Pour in onion mixture. Sprinkle with almonds.

5. Place covered cooker in cold oven. Set oven at 400°F (200°C). Bake until soufflé is puffed and golden brown, about 45 minutes. Serve immediately.

Curried Cauliflower with Peas

1/2	teaspoon (2 mL) mustard seeds
2	tablespoons (30 mL) vegetable oil
1	medium onion, finely chopped
1	teaspoon (5 mL) pared, grated fresh ginger root, or 1/4 teaspoon (1 mL) ground ginger
1	teaspoon (5 mL) salt
1	teaspoon (5 mL) ground cumin
1/2	teaspoon (2 mL) ground turmeric
1/4	teaspoon (1 mL) cayenne pepper
1/4	cup (60 mL) water
1	medium cauliflower (about 1 1/4 pounds or 550 g), separated into small flowerettes
1	cup (250 mL) frozen peas, thawed

Cauliflower and peas, cooked with an Indian-influenced seasoning mixture, make a colorful accompaniment for chicken or lamb. Stir in the peas just at the end to keep them spring green.

1. Soak top and bottom of 2-quart (2 L) clay cooker in water about 15 minutes; drain.

2. Cook mustard seeds in oil in medium skillet until seeds begin to pop. Stir in onions; cook, stirring occasionally, until light brown. Stir in ginger root, salt, cumin, turmeric and cayenne; remove from heat. Stir in water.

3. Place cauliflower pieces in cooker; add onion mixture.

4. Place covered cooker in cold oven. Set oven at 475°F (250°C). Bake, stirring once, just until cauliflower is tender, 20 to 30 minutes. Stir in peas; cook covered until peas are hot, about 5 minutes.

Scalloped Onions with Poppy Seeds

2	tablespoons (30 mL) butter or margarine, melted
8	medium onions (about 2 pounds or 900 g), thinly sliced
2	tablespoons (30 mL) poppy seeds
1	teaspoon (5 mL) salt
1/4	teaspoon (1 mL) white pepper
2	packages (each 3 ounces or 85 g) cream cheese, room temperature
2/3	cup (160 mL) half-and-half

Ordinarily used to season other foods, here onions play a starring role. Crunchy with poppy seeds, this dish turns crustily pan-fried ground beef patties into an elegant meal.

1. Soak top and bottom of 3 1/4-quart (3.25 L) clay cooker in water about 15 minutes; drain.

2. Pat dry and brush sides and bottom of cooker with melted butter. Place half the onions in cooker; sprinkle with half the poppy seeds, half the salt and half the pepper. Add remaining onions; sprinkle with remaining poppy seeds, salt and pepper.

3. Heat cream cheese in small saucepan over low heat until melted. Stir in half-and-half gradually; stir until smooth. Pour over onions.

4. Place covered cooker in cold oven. Set oven at 425°F (220°C). Bake, stirring once or twice, until onions are tender and sauce is thick, about 1 1/4 hours. Remove cover; bake until top browns, about 10 minutes.

Makes 8 servings

Potatoes Anna

1/2   **cup (125 mL) butter or margarine**
6   **large baking potatoes (about 4 pounds or 1800 g), pared, very thinly sliced**
     Salt
     White pepper

The charm of this classic French dish is in unmolding it perfectly into a crusty golden potato cake. However, if that sort of sleight-of-hand seems risky, these potatoes can be appreciated spooned directly from the clay cooker. Before baking, the potatoes should fill the cooker right to the brim; as they cook they shrink into a less formidable volume.

1. Soak top and bottom of 2-quart (2 L) clay cooker in water about 15 minutes; drain. (If desired, you may line cooker with parchment paper cut to fit bottom to facilitate unmolding.)

2. Melt butter in small saucepan. Pat dry and brush bottom and sides of cooker generously with some of the butter. Arrange single layer of sliced potatoes over bottom and around sides of cooker, overlapping slices slightly. Sprinkle lightly with salt and pepper. Arrange remaining potatoes in thin horizontal layers, sprinkling each layer with salt, pepper and butter. Pour remaining butter over top.

3. Place covered cooker in cold oven. Set oven at 425°F (220°C). Bake until potatoes are tender in the center, crusty and brown, about 1 1/2 hours. Remove cover; bake until top browns, 5 to 10 minutes. Loosen edges with spatula; invert onto warm serving platter.

Makes 4 servings

Zucchini with Tomato Sauce

---

2   **small tomatoes, peeled, chopped**
1   **small onion, chopped**
1   **clove garlic, minced**
1/2   **teaspoon (2 mL) dried basil leaves**
1/4   **teaspoon (1 mL) sugar**
1/4   **teaspoon (1 mL) dried oregano leaves**
1/2   **teaspoon (2 mL) salt**
     Pinch pepper
1/4   **cup (60 mL) dry white wine**
2   **tablespoons (30 mL) tomato paste**
1   **tablespoon (15 mL) olive or vegetable oil**
4   **medium zucchini (about 1 1/4 pounds or 550 g), unpeeled, cut into 1/4-inch (0.5 cm) slices**

Tomato sauce cooks to thick richness in the clay cooker. Zucchini is added just at the end to retain its bright green color and a gentle crispness.

1. Soak top and bottom of 2-quart (2 L) clay cooker in water about 15 minutes; drain.

2. Combine all ingredients, except zucchini, in cooker.

3. Place covered cooker in cold oven. Set oven at 425°F (220°C). Bake, stirring once or twice, until sauce is thick, about 1 hour.

4. Stir in zucchini. Bake covered until zucchini is crisp-tender, 20 to 25 minutes.

Broccoli au Gratin

Makes 4 to 6 servings

2   tablespoons (30 mL) butter or
    margarine, melted
4   cups (1 L) small fresh broccoli
    flowerettes and thinly sliced
    stems
1/4 cup (60 mL) finely chopped
    onion
1   egg
1/3 cup (80 mL) whipping cream
1/4 cup (60 mL) regular-strength
    chicken broth, canned or
    homemade
1/4 teaspoon (1 mL) salt
    Pinch white pepper
1/8 teaspoon (0.5 mL) ground
    nutmeg
1/2 cup (125 mL) fresh bread
    crumbs
1/4 cup (60 mL) shredded Cheddar
    cheese

*The first burst of steam created within a soaked clay cooker in the oven is
enough to cook many green vegetables. Try this technique for broccoli in a
custard-like cream. A crisp topping of buttered crumbs and cheese is added
during the last few minutes of baking.*

1. Soak top and bottom of 2-quart (2 L) clay cooker in water about 15
minutes; drain.

2. Pat dry and brush bottom and sides of cooker with 1 tablespoon (15 mL) of
the butter. Add broccoli and onion. Beat egg, cream, broth, salt, pepper and
nutmeg; pour over broccoli.

3. Place covered cooker in cold oven. Set oven at 425°F (220°C). Bake just
until broccoli is tender and custard is set, 25 to 30 minutes.

4. Combine remaining butter, the bread crumbs and cheese. Sprinkle evenly
over broccoli. Bake uncovered until crumbs are crisp and brown, about 5
minutes.

Herbed Spinach Casserole

Makes 6 servings

2   bunches spinach (about 1
     pound or 450 g)
1/3 cup (80 mL) milk
2   tablespoons (30 mL) butter or
     margarine, melted
1/2 teaspoon (2 mL)
     Worcestershire sauce
2   eggs
1   small onion, finely chopped
1   tablespoon (15 mL) minced
     fresh parsley
1   teaspoon (5 mL) salt
1/4 teaspoon (1 mL) dried thyme
     leaves
1/4 teaspoon (1 mL) ground
     nutmeg
1   cup (250 mL) cooked white
     rice
1 1/2 cups (375 mL) shredded Swiss
     cheese

*Most people will enjoy this casserole as a lively accompaniment to simply
cooked meats; but, if you wish, it can be a meatless main dish, accompanied by
sliced tomatoes and a twisted egg bread.*

1. Soak top and bottom of 3 1/4-quart (3.25 L) clay cooker in water about 15
minutes; drain.

2. Rinse spinach thoroughly; remove and discard stems. Place leaves in
cooker.

3. Place covered cooker in cold oven. Set oven at 425°F (220°C). Bake,
stirring once, until spinach is wilted and just tender, about 15 minutes; drain
well. Coarsely chop spinach.

4. While spinach is cooking, beat milk, butter, Worcestershire sauce, eggs,
onion, parsley, salt, thyme and nutmeg until blended.

5. Place spinach, rice and 1 cup (250 mL) of the cheese in cooker. Stir in egg
mixture gently. Sprinkle with remaining cheese. Bake covered 20 minutes.
Remove cover; bake until top is light brown, about 10 minutes.

Corn Spoon Bread

2   cups (500 mL) milk
3/4 cup (180 mL) yellow cornmeal
3   tablespoons (45 mL) butter or
     margarine
3/4 teaspoon (4 mL) salt
4   eggs, separated
1   cup (250 mL) frozen corn,
     thawed
1/8 teaspoon (0.5 mL) cream of
     tartar
     Melted butter or margarine, if
     desired

Resembling a moist, light cornbread, you might serve this spoon bread with baked ham. Or, make it part of a main dish by serving it as a foundation for creamed chipped beef, ham or chicken.

1. Soak top and bottom of 2-quart (2 L) clay cooker in water about 15 minutes; drain.

2. Scald milk in medium saucepan; stir in cornmeal gradually. Cook over medium heat, stirring constantly, until very thick; remove from heat. Stir in 2 tablespoons (30 mL) of the butter and the salt. Let stand until slightly cooled.

3. Melt remaining butter; pat dry and brush sides and bottom of cooker with butter.

4. Beat egg yolks, one at a time, into cornmeal mixture. Stir in corn. Beat egg whites and cream of tartar until peaks are short and distinct when beaters are raised. Fold egg whites gently into cornmeal mixture. Pour into cooker.

5. Place covered cooker in cold oven. Set oven at 400°F (200°C). Bake until puffed and golden brown, about 45 minutes. Serve immediately with melted butter poured over each serving.

Mexican Red Rice

2   tablespoons (30 mL) butter or
     margarine, melted
1   cup (250 mL) uncooked long-
     grain white rice
1/2 cup (125 mL) coarsely chopped
     ripe olives
1   medium onion, finely chopped
1   clove garlic, minced
1/2 teaspoon (2 mL) salt
1/2 teaspoon (2 mL) ground cumin
     Pinch cayenne pepper
1   can (8 ounces or 225 g) tomato
     sauce
1½   cups (375 mL) regular-strength
     chicken broth, canned or
     homemade
1½   cups (375 mL) shredded
     Monterey Jack cheese

South-of-the-border flavors accent this rice casserole. It is enjoyable with a meat loaf or baked chicken and a tossed salad.

1. Soak top and bottom of 2-quart (2 L) clay cooker in water about 15 minutes; drain.

2. Pat dry and brush sides and bottom of cooker with butter. Combine rice, olives, onion, garlic, salt, cumin, cayenne, tomato sauce and chicken broth in cooker.

3. Place covered cooker in cold oven. Set oven at 425°F (220°C). Bake until rice is almost tender, about 45 minutes.

4. Stir in 1 cup (250 mL) of the cheese; sprinkle with remaining cheese. Bake uncovered until cheese melts and browns, about 10 minutes.

Mrs. B's Baked Beans

Makes 6 servings

1   pound (450 g) dried pinto
     beans, rinsed, drained
6   cups (1.5 L) water
1/2 pound (225 g) salt pork, cut
     into 1/4-inch (0.5 cm) slices
1   medium onion, thinly sliced,
     separated into rings
1/4 cup (60 mL) dark molasses
3   tablespoons (45 mL) brown
     sugar
3/4 teaspoon (4 mL) dry mustard

Similar to Boston baked beans, but made with speckled pinto beans, this dish makes a fine contribution to a cooperative picnic or potluck supper.

1. The day before cooking beans, place beans in a large bowl; add water. Let stand overnight. [Or, heat beans and water in 4-quart (4 L) kettle to boiling; boil briskly 2 minutes. Remove from heat. Let stand covered 1 hour.]

2. Soak top and bottom of 3 1/4-quart (3.25 L) clay cooker in water about 15 minutes; drain.

3. Arrange half the salt pork in bottom of cooker; top with half the onions. Add half the beans. Cover with remaining salt pork and onions. Add remaining beans and the cooking liquid. Mix molasses, brown sugar and mustard. Drizzle over beans.

4. Place covered cooker in cold oven. Set oven at 375°F (190°C). Bake, stirring once every hour, until beans are tender, about 4 hours.

Tomato-Cheese Soufflé

Makes 6 servings

1   large can (28 ounces or 800 g)
     tomatoes, coarsely chopped,
     liquid reserved
1   medium onion, finely chopped
1   clove garlic, minced
1/2 teaspoon (2 mL) sugar
1/4 teaspoon (1 mL) dried basil
     leaves
1   teaspoon (5 mL) salt
1/4 teaspoon (1 mL) freshly ground
     pepper
1/4 cup (60 mL) butter or
     margarine
1/4 cup (60 mL) all-purpose flour
1   cup (250 mL) shredded
     Monterey Jack cheese
6   eggs, separated
1/8 teaspoon (0.5 mL) cream of
     tartar

The brilliant red-orange color of this silken soufflé makes it a favorite menu brightener for winter meals with fish or chicken.

1. Soak top and bottom of 2-quart (2 L) clay cooker in water about 15 minutes; drain

2. Combine tomatoes with liquid, onion, garlic, sugar, basil, salt and pepper in large saucepan. Heat to boiling; cook, stirring frequently until reduced to 1 3/4 cups (450 mL). Process in blender or food processor until smooth.

3. Melt butter in large saucepan; remove and reserve 1 tablespoon (15 mL) of the butter. Add flour to saucepan; cook, stirring constantly, until bubbly. Remove from heat; stir in tomato mixture gradually. Cook, stirring constantly, until thickened. Stir in 3/4 cup (180 mL) of the cheese until melted; remove from heat. Beat in egg yolks.

4. Beat egg whites and cream of tartar until peaks are short and distinct when beaters are lifted. Fold egg whites into tomato mixture. Pat dry and brush bottom and sides of cooker with reserved butter. Pour in soufflé mixture. Sprinkle with remaining cheese.

5. Place covered cooker in cold oven. Set oven at 400°F (200°C). Bake until soufflé is puffed and brown, 40 to 45 minutes. Serve immediately.

Rice-Stuffed Tomatoes

Makes 4 servings

2   tablespoons (30 mL) olive oil
1/3 cup (80 mL) uncooked long-
     grain white rice
1   small onion, finely chopped
1   clove garlic, minced
1/4 teaspoon (1 mL) dried thyme
     leaves
1/2 teaspoon (2 mL) salt
1/8 teaspoon (0.5 mL) pepper
2/3 cup (160 mL) regular-strength
     chicken broth, canned or
     homemade
4   medium tomatoes
     Salt
2   tablespoons (30 mL) minced
     fresh parsley
1/4 cup (60 mL) shredded Cheddar
     cheese.

First cook the herbed rice stuffing in the clay cooker (lining it with parchment paper for easy removal), then use it to fill hollowed-out tomatoes. Topped with cheese, they are a fine foil for grilled lamb chops or can be a luncheon main dish with thinly sliced cold meats and crisp hard rolls.

1. Soak top and bottom of 2-quart (2 L) clay cooker in water about 15 minutes; drain. Line bottom and sides of cooker with parchment paper. Brush parchment paper with olive oil.

2. Combine rice, onion, garlic, thyme, salt, pepper and broth; add to cooker.

3. Place covered cooker in cold oven. Set oven at 425°F (220°C). Bake just until rice is tender, about 45 minutes.

4. While rice is cooking; cut 1/2-inch (1.5 cm) slice from stem end of each tomato; reserve slices. Scoop out centers of tomatoes; reserve pulp. Remove and discard seeds. Sprinkle insides of tomatoes lightly with salt; invert onto paper toweling. Chop reserved tomato slices and pulp.

5. Remove parchment paper with rice from cooker. Stir chopped tomato and the parsley into rice. Fill tomato shells with rice mixture; place in cooker.

6. Bake covered for 10 minutes. Sprinkle tomatoes with cheese. Bake uncovered until cheese melts and browns, about 10 minutes.

Braised Belgian Endive

Makes 4 to 6 servings

1   pound (450 g) small Belgian
     endives (8 to 10)
2   tablespoons (30 mL) butter or
     margarine, room
     temperature
2   teaspoons (10 mL) lemon juice
     Salt
     White pepper
1   cup (250 mL) regular-strength
     chicken broth, canned or
     homemade

One of the most elegant of vegetables, Braised Belgian Endive in a lemony sauce is lovely with a simple roast chicken or poached fish.

1. Soak top and bottom of 5 1/2-cup to 2-quart (1375 mL to 2 L) clay cooker in water about 15 minutes; drain.

2. Trim ends of endives and remove discolored outer leaves. Place endives in cooker. Dot with butter. Sprinkle with lemon juice, salt and pepper. Pour in chicken broth.

3. Place covered cooker in cold oven. Set oven at 425°F (220°C). Bake until endives are tender, about 45 minutes. Pour cooking liquid into medium saucepan; cover cooker to keep endive warm.

4. Heat cooking liquid to boiling; cook, stirring occasionally, until syrupy. Pour over endive.

Celery Parmigiana

Makes 6 servings

1   bunch celery, (1¹/₂ to 2 pounds
        or 675 to 900 g)
1   cup (250 mL) water
¹/₂ teaspoon (2 mL) salt
¹/₄ cup (60 mL) butter or
        margarine, melted
¹/₄ cup (60 mL) whipping cream
¹/₂ cup (125 mL) grated Parmesan
        cheese

Cooked in clay, celery retains its distinctive flavor and delightful crispness. A buttery cream sauce makes the dish a perfect partner for a crisp-skinned roast chicken or sautéed veal with a squeeze of lemon.

1. Soak top and bottom of 3¹/₄-quart (3.25 L) clay cooker in water about 15 minutes; drain.

2. Cut tops and bottoms from celery. Cut ribs diagonally into ¹/₂-inch (1.5 cm) pieces. Place in cooker; add water and salt.

3. Place covered cooker in cold oven. Set oven at 425°F (220°C). Bake until celery is almost tender, 35 to 40 minutes; drain.

4. Mix butter and cream; pour into cooker. Sprinkle celery with Parmesan cheese. Bake uncovered until celery is tender and top is light brown, about 15 minutes.

Swiss Chard with Onions

Makes 4 servings

2   medium onions, thinly sliced,
        separated into rings
2   tablespoons (30 mL) butter or
        margarine
1   clove garlic, minced
1   large bunch Swiss chard (about
        1 pound or 450 g), coarsely
        chopped (about 6 cups or
        1.5 L)
     Salt
     Pepper
1   teaspoon (5 mL) lemon juice

Arranged over a bed of sweetly sautéed onions, chard steams in its own moisture in a clay cooker to an appealing savor. Italian in origin, this dish complements baked chicken or grilled, herb-buttered steak.

1. Soak top and bottom of 3¹/₄-quart (3.25 L) clay cooker in water about 15 minutes; drain.

2. Sauté onions in butter in large skillet over medium heat, stirring occasionally, until limp and beginning to brown; stir in garlic. Spread onion mixture in bottom of cooker. Add chard.

3. Place covered cooker in cold oven. Set oven at 425°F (220°C). Bake, stirring once, until chard is crisp-tender, 20 to 25 minutes.

4. Season with salt, pepper and lemon juice.

Garlic Buttered Brussels Sprouts

Makes 4 servings

1   pound (450 g) fresh Brussels
        sprouts
¹/₄ teaspoon (1 mL) salt
¹/₄ cup (60 mL) water
1   clove garlic, minced

Those who think they don't like Brussels sprouts may think twice when this vegetable is served in a lusty garlic butter. Clay cooking leaves the sprouts tasting surprisingly sweet.

1. Soak top and bottom of 2-quart (2 L) clay cooker in water about 15 minutes; drain.

GARLIC BUTTERED BRUSSELS SPROUTS, continued

1/4	cup (60 mL) butter or margarine
1	teaspoon (5 mL) lemon juice

2. Remove loose and discolored leaves from Brussels sprouts. Trim stem ends; cut an X in each end. Place Brussels sprouts in cooker. Sprinkle with salt. Pour in water.

3. Place covered cooker in cold oven. Set oven at 425°F (220°C). Bake just until sprouts are tender, 25 to 30 minutes.

4. Sauté garlic in butter in small skillet until light brown; stir in lemon juice; remove from heat. Drain Brussels sprouts; drizzle with garlic butter.

Makes 4 to 6 servings

Scalloped Mushrooms

1	pound (450 g) mushrooms, sliced
	Salt
	Freshly ground pepper
2	cups (500 mL) fresh French bread crumbs
1/2	cup (125 mL) butter or margarine, melted
1/4	cup (60 mL) dry white wine

With a grilled steak or rare beef roast, nothing is quite as elegant as wine-scented mushrooms with a buttery crumb topping.

1. Soak top and bottom of 3 1/4-quart (3.25 L) clay cooker in water about 15 minutes; drain.

2. Place half the mushrooms in cooker; sprinkle generously with salt and pepper. Top with half the bread crumbs; drizzle half the butter over bread crumbs. Top with remaining mushrooms; sprinkle with salt and pepper. Pour in wine.

3. Place covered cooker in cold oven. Set oven at 425°F (220°C). Bake until mushrooms are tender, about 30 minutes. Mix remaining bread crumbs and butter; sprinkle over mushrooms. Bake uncovered until crumbs are brown, 8 to 10 minutes.

Makes 6 servings

Saffron Rice Pilaf

2	tablespoons (30 mL) butter or margarine, melted
1	cup (250 mL) uncooked long-grain white rice
1	small onion, finely chopped
1	clove garlic, minced
1/4	teaspoon (1 mL) salt
	Pinch white pepper
1/8	teaspoon (0.5 mL) dried saffron threads or powdered saffron
1	can (13 3/4 ounces or 385 g) regular-strength chicken broth
1/4	cup (60 mL) dry white wine
1/2	cup (125 mL) freshly grated Parmesan cheese

To accompany your favorite saucy Italian dish, such as Italian Veal Shanks (see Index for page number), here is a brilliant, golden rice dish traditional in Milan.

1. Soak top and bottom of 5 1/2-cup to 2-quart (1375 mL to 2 L) clay cooker in water about 15 minutes; drain.

2. Pat dry and brush sides and bottom of cooker with butter. Combine rice, onion, garlic, salt, pepper, saffron, broth and wine in cooker.

3. Place covered cooker in cold oven. Set oven at 425°F (220°C). Bake until rice is tender, 45 to 50 minutes.

4. Stir in cheese; serve immediately.

Makes 6 to 8 servings

Ratatouille

1 **medium eggplant (about 1¹/₄ pounds or 550 g), unpared, cut into ¹/₂-inch (1.5 cm) cubes**
2 **teaspoons (10 mL) salt**
3 **medium zucchini (about 1 pound or 450 g), unpared, cut into ³/₄-inch (2 cm) slices**
2 **medium onions, thinly sliced, separated into rings**
3 **cloves garlic, minced**
2 **green or red bell peppers, cut into 1-inch (2.5 cm) squares**
1 **teaspoon (5 mL) dried basil leaves**
¹/₄ **cup (60 mL) minced fresh parsley**
1 **large can (28 ounces or 800 g) tomatoes, coarsely chopped, liquid reserved**
¹/₄ **cup (60 mL) olive oil Minced fresh parsley**

The appeal of this vegetable dish is as much in its musical name, as in the colorful melange of vegetables. The nice feature of this clay cooker interpretation is that the vegetables stay in distinct pieces and still develop savory flavor as they bake. Serve Ratatouille hot, at room temperature or chilled. Any leftovers make a good meatless main dish reheated in individual casseroles with a topping of shredded Swiss or Gruyère cheese.

1. Spread eggplant cubes in single layer on paper toweling. Sprinkle with salt; let stand 20 minutes. Pat dry with paper toweling.

2. Soak top and bottom of 3¹/₄-quart (3.25 L) clay cooker in water about 15 minutes; drain.

3. Place eggplant in cooker. Layer remaining ingredients, except olive oil and minced parsley for garnish, over eggplant. Drizzle oil over top.

4. Place covered cooker in cold oven. Set oven at 400°F (200°C). Bake, basting top two or three times with cooking liquid, 3 hours.

5. Remove cover; bake until Ratatouille is no longer soupy, 10 to 15 minutes. Stir gently to combine ingredients. Garnish with parsley.

Makes 4 servings

Cream Glazed Green Beans

1 **pound (450 g) fresh green beans**
2 **tablespoons (30 mL) butter or margarine**
¹/₄ **cup (60 mL) water**
¹/₄ **cup (60 mL) whipping cream**
¹/₈ **teaspoon (0.5 mL) paprika**
2 **tablespoons (30 mL) freshly grated Parmesan cheese Salt**

Tender-crisp whole beans are served with a creamy sauce made by reducing their cooking liquid with cream. This vegetable is a perfect accompaniment for roast lamb.

1. Soak top and bottom of 2-quart (2 L) clay cooker in water about 15 minutes; drain.

2. Snap off ends and remove strings from beans. Place beans in cooker; dot with butter; add the water.

3. Place covered cooker in cold oven at 475°F (250°C). Bake just until beans are tender, 25 to 35 minutes.

4. Drain cooking liquid into medium saucepan. Cover cooker to keep beans warm. Add cream and paprika to cooking liquid. Boil, stirring occasionally, until reduced and slightly thickened. Stir in cheese. Taste and add salt as needed.

5. Toss beans with cream sauce.

VEGETABLES

Jansson's Temptation

Makes 6 servings

4   tablespoons (60 mL) butter or margarine, melted
4   medium new boiling potatoes (about 2 pounds or 900 g), pared, thinly sliced
1   medium onion, thinly sliced, separated into rings
1   can (2 ounces or 60 g) flat anchovy fillets, drained
1   cup (250 mL) whipping cream

No one knows the identity of Jansson, who gave his name to this creamy scalloped potato dish. But almost everyone finds its salty zest of anchovies seductive.

1. Soak top and bottom of 3 1/4-quart (3.25 L) clay cooker in water about 15 minutes; drain.

2. Pat dry and brush sides and bottom of cooker with 1 tablespoon (15 mL) of the butter. Arrange half the potatoes in layers in cooker; top with onions. Drizzle half the remaining butter over onions. Arrange anchovies over onions. Cover with remaining potatoes. Drizzle remaining butter over potatoes. Pour in cream.

3. Place covered cooker in cold oven. Set oven at 425°F (220°C). Bake until potatoes are tender at center, about 1 hour. Remove cover; bake until top browns, 8 to 10 minutes.

German Sweet-Sour Red Cabbage

Makes 6 to 8 servings

1   head red cabbage (about 2 pounds or 900 g), shredded
2   tart apples, pared, cored, shredded
4   whole cloves
1 1/2 tablespoons (22 mL) sugar
1 1/2 teaspoons (7 mL) salt
1/3 cup (80 mL) white wine vinegar
1   cup (250 mL) water
2   tablespoons (30 mL) butter or margarine
   Minced fresh parsley

With Sauerbraten (see Index for page number), nothing will suffice but a tart, sweet-sour red cabbage. Here is a version for your clay cooker. A food processor makes quick work of shredding the cabbage and apples.

1. Soak top and bottom of 3 1/4-quart (3.25 L) clay cooker in water about 15 minutes; drain. Line bottom and sides of cooker with parchment paper.

2. Combine cabbage, apples, cloves, sugar and salt in clay cooker. Drizzle with vinegar. Pour in water. Dot with butter.

3. Place covered cooker in cold oven. Set oven at 375°F (190°C). Bake, stirring once or twice during last hour, until most of the liquid has evaporated, 2 to 2 1/2 hours. Garnish with parsley.

Ginger Glazed Carrots

Makes 4 to 6 servings

6   medium carrots (about 1 1/2 pounds or 675 g), pared
1/4 cup (60 mL) water
1/4 teaspoon (1 mL) salt
3   tablespoons (45 mL) butter or margarine
1/4 cup (60 mL) packed brown sugar
1/2 teaspoon (2 mL) ground ginger

Glistening carrots accompany a holiday turkey or pork roast stylishly.

1. Soak top and bottom of 2-quart (2 L) clay cooker in water about 15 minutes; drain.

2. Cut carrots lengthwise into quarters. Place carrots in cooker; add water; sprinkle with salt.

108

GINGER GLAZED CARROTS, continued

3. Place covered cooker in cold oven. Set oven at 425°F (220°C). Bake, stirring once or twice, until carrots are tender, 35 to 40 minutes. Drain.

4. Melt butter in small skillet. Stir in brown sugar and ginger; cook, stirring constantly, until bubbly. Drizzle butter mixture over carrots.

5. Bake uncovered, carefully turning carrots once, until glazed, about 5 minutes.

Spiced Baked Squash with Apples

Makes 4 servings

2 small acorn squash (each about 1 pound or 450 g)
1 tart red apple, unpared, cored, thinly sliced
2 tablespoons (30 mL) butter or margarine
2 tablespoons (30 mL) brown sugar
1/4 teaspoon (1 mL) ground ginger
1/8 teaspoon (0.5 mL) ground cloves

An autumn favorite, baked acorn squash is a colorful side dish to serve with ham or pork chops.

1. Soak top and bottom of square 2-quart (2 L) clay cooker in water about 15 minutes; drain.

2. Cut squash lengthwise in half; scoop out and discard seeds. Place squash, cut side up, in cooker. Divide apple slices into hollows of squash. Dot with butter. Mix brown sugar, ginger and cloves; sprinkle over apples.

3. Place covered cooker in cold oven. Set oven at 425°F (220°C). Bake until squash is tender, about 1 hour. Spoon cooking liquid over squash.

Hazel's Puffy Baked Rutabaga

Makes 6 to 8 servings

2 medium rutabagas (about 2³/4 pounds or 1250 g), pared, diced
1 cup (250 mL) water
1/2 teaspoon (2 mL) salt
1/4 cup (60 mL) half-and-half
2 eggs
2 tablespoons (30 mL) flour
1/2 teaspoon (2 mL) seasoned salt
1/8 teaspoon (0.5 mL) white pepper
1/8 teaspoon (0.5 mL) ground cinnamon
2 tablespoons (30 mL) butter or margarine, melted

The earthy taste of rutabaga is softened by beating the cooked vegetable into a fluff with a hint of cinnamon. Eggs give it an almost soufflé-like lightness.

1. Soak top and bottom of 2-quart (2 L) clay cooker in water about 15 minutes; drain.

2. Place rutabagas, water and salt in cooker.

3. Place covered cooker in cold oven. Set oven at 425°F (220°C). Bake until rutabagas are very tender, 45 to 50 minutes; drain.

4. Place rutabagas in medium mixer bowl; add half-and-half, eggs, flour, seasoned salt, pepper and cinnamon. Beat until smooth and fluffy. Pat dry and brush bottom and sides of cooker with butter. Spread rutabaga mixture in cooker.

5. Bake covered 15 minutes. Remove cover; bake until top begins to brown, about 10 minutes.

Microwave Cooking in Clay

Combining an ancient style of cooking with the most modern kitchen technology—the microwave oven—is not at all bizarre. In fact, they team up perfectly. Using your clay cooker in a microwave oven can result in greater tenderness for less choice cuts of meat—the kind that need slow, moist-heat cooking. You may also find that clay cooking helps to increase browning and seems to bring out more flavor in microwaved foods.

A microwave oven with variable power can give your clay cooker greater flexibility in cooking less tender meats, rice and pasta, using a low-power or simmer setting. For chicken and most vegetables, you can set your microwave oven at full power.

For microwave cooking, soak your clay cooker as usual. The moisture absorbed by the clay will produce two noticeable effects. The clay cooker will get somewhat warmer than a glass bowl or casserole, because the water in the clay absorbs microwave energy; and cooking times will be somewhat longer.

Don't let either of these phenomena dissuade you. Manufacturers of clay cookers and of microwave ovens recognize the benefits to be gained by cooking in clay with microwaves and both recommend the combination.

Remember the techniques you use to promote more even microwave cooking in other containers, and take advantage of them when you cook in clay. Arrange foods so that thicker, meatier parts are at the ends, corners and outside edges of the clay cooker. Meats or poultry with bones will cook better if turned end-over-end at least once. Food in the very center will be the last part to cook, so stir the center portion outward, if possible, after half to two-thirds of the cooking time has elapsed.

If you have observed that food in one spot in your microwave oven tends to cook more rapidly, give the clay cooker several quarter or half turns to achieve more even cooking.

You have probably noticed that many foods cooked by microwaves need a brief standing period before serving. This is also true when you use your clay cooker. Learn to undercook slightly, then keep the cover on for up to half an hour. The clay holds heat inside to complete cooking and to keep food hot until you are ready to serve it.

Makes 6 servings

Beef Stew with Vegetables

2¼ to 2½ pounds (1050 to 1125 g) boneless beef chuck, cut into 1-inch (2.5 cm) cubes, fat trimmed
2 tablespoons (30 mL) flour
1½ teaspoons (7 mL) salt
⅛ teaspoon (0.5 mL) seasoned pepper
½ teaspoon (2 mL) paprika
2 medium carrots, pared, cut diagonally into ½-inch (1.5 cm) slices
½ pound (225 g) mushrooms, cut into quarters
2 medium onions, thinly sliced
2 cloves garlic, minced
½ cup (125 mL) water
¼ cup (60 mL) chili sauce
1 beef bouillon cube
Chopped fresh parsley

A traditional stew with carrots, mushrooms and onions browns richly and becomes fork-tender using medium-low microwave power for about an hour's cooking time. Accompany the stew with baked potatoes. If you wish to bake them in the microwave oven, put them in the oven after the stew is cooked. The stew will stay warm at room temperature in the covered clay cooker.

1. Soak top and bottom of 3¼-quart (3.25 L) clay cooker in water about 15 minutes; drain.

2. Coat beef cubes with mixture of flour, salt, pepper and paprika. Place in cooker.

3. Place covered cooker in microwave oven. Microwave on full power 15 minutes; turn beef cubes. Add remaining ingredients except parsley. Microwave covered on medium-low power (simmer), stirring once or twice, until meat and vegetables are tender, 50 to 60 minutes. Garnish with parsley.

Makes 6 servings

Shrimp and Italian Sausage Risotto

1 pound (450 g) mild Italian pork sausages, casings removed
1 medium onion, finely chopped
1 clove garlic, minced
1 cup (250 mL) uncooked long-grain white rice
1 can (13¾ ounces or 400 g) regular-strength chicken broth
¾ cup (180 mL) dry white wine
½ cup (125 mL) shredded Parmesan cheese
1 pound (450 g) raw shrimp, shelled, deveined
Minced fresh parsley

Served with lightly sautéed zucchini, crisp bread sticks and a basket of cherry tomatoes, this elegant rice dish makes a fine company supper. Accompany with a well chilled dry Chablis.

1. Soak top and bottom of 3¼-quart (3.25 L) clay cooker in water about 15 minutes; drain.

2. Crumble sausages into cooker.

3. Place covered cooker in microwave oven. Microwave on full power, stirring once, until sausage loses pink color (about 8 minutes). Pour off and discard drippings. Stir in onion and garlic; microwave covered on full power 3 minutes. Stir in rice, broth and wine; microwave covered on low power (defrost) just until rice is tender, 40 to 45 minutes.

4. Stir in cheese. Arrange shrimp, tails at center, in even layer over rice. Microwave covered on full power until shrimp turns pink, about 5 minutes.

5. Let stand covered about 5 minutes. Garnish with parsley.

Makes 6 to 8 servings

Fruited Country-Style Spareribs

4 pounds (1800 g) country-style spareribs, cut into serving pieces
1 medium onion, finely chopped
1 clove garlic, minced
12 pitted prunes
1/2 cup (125 mL) dried apricots
1 lemon, thinly sliced
1 piece cinnamon stick, 2 inches (5 cm) long
1 tablespoon (15 mL) brown sugar
1 teaspoon (5 mL) salt
1/2 teaspoon (2 mL) ground ginger
1/2 cup (125 mL) regular-strength beef broth, canned or homemade
1 1/2 tablespoons (22 mL) Worcestershire sauce
1 tablespoon (15 mL) soy sauce
2 teaspoons (10 mL) cornstarch
1 tablespoon (15 mL) water

Lemon, prunes, dried apricots and spices add a delicious savor to these moist, meaty spareribs from the pork loin.

1. Soak top and bottom of 3 1/4-quart (3.25 L) clay cooker in water about 15 minutes; drain.

2. Place spareribs in cooker. Sprinkle with onion and garlic. Cover with even layer of prunes and apricots; layer lemon slices over fruit. Insert cinnamon stick near center. Mix brown sugar, salt and ginger; sprinkle over lemon slices. Mix broth, Worcestershire sauce and soy sauce; pour into cooker.

3. Place covered cooker in microwave oven. Microwave on full power 20 minutes; reduce power to medium-low (simmer). Microwave covered, rearranging spareribs once, until spareribs are tender, about 45 minutes.

4. Remove spareribs to warm serving bowl; keep warm. Skim and discard fat from cooking liquid. Mix cornstarch and water; stir into cooking liquid. Microwave on full power until sauce bubbles and thickens, about 3 minutes. Stir sauce with fruit and pour over spareribs.

Makes 6 servings

Baked Lentils with Smoky Sausages

1 package (12 ounces or 340 g) lentils, rinsed, drained
1 large can (16 fluid ounces or 500 mL) beer
1 beef bouillon cube
1 large can (15 ounces or 425 g) tomato sauce
1 medium onion, finely chopped
1 bay leaf
1/3 cup (80 mL) packed brown sugar
2 tablespoons (30 mL) dark molasses
1 tablespoon (15 mL) prepared mustard
1 cup (250 mL) water
1 package (12 ounces or 340 g) smoked link sausages

With flavors reminiscent of baked beans, this sausage-topped lentil casserole makes a good family meal served with crisp vegetable relishes and warm brown bread.

1. Soak top and bottom of 3 1/4-quart (3.25 L) clay cooker in water about 15 minutes; drain.

2. Combine all ingredients except water and sausages in cooker.

3. Place covered cooker in microwave oven. Microwave on full power 15 minutes; stir in water. Microwave covered on medium-low power (simmer), stirring once or twice, until lentils are tender, about 1 1/4 to 1 1/2 hours.

4. Pierce each sausage in several places with fork; arrange over lentils. Microwave covered until sausages are plump and hot, 3 to 5 minutes. Let stand covered about 5 minutes before serving.

Tuna and Shells Casserole

Makes 4 to 6 servings

1   tablespoon (15 mL) olive or vegetable oil
1   medium onion, finely chopped
1   rib celery, finely chopped
1   clove garlic, minced
1   large can (28 ounces or 800 g) Italian-style plum tomatoes, coarsely chopped, liquid reserved
1/2 cup (125 mL) dry white wine
1   cup (250 mL) small macaroni shells
1/2 teaspoon (2 mL) salt
1/2 teaspoon (2 mL) mixed Italian herbs
1/4 teaspoon (1 mL) lemon pepper
1   large can (9 1/4 ounces or 275 g) chunk light tuna, drained, flaked
1/4 cup (60 mL) minced fresh parsley
1   cup (250 mL) shredded Monterey Jack cheese
1/4 cup (60 mL) grated Parmesan cheese

Accompany this hearty tuna and tomato casserole with broccoli spears and hot, buttery garlic bread.

1. Soak top and bottom of 3 1/4-quart (3.25 L) clay cooker in water about 15 minutes; drain.

2. Combine olive oil, onion, celery and garlic in cooker. Microwave covered on full power until vegetables are limp, 8 to 10 minutes. Stir in tomatoes with liquid and wine. Microwave uncovered on full power until fully boiling, 12 to 15 minutes. Stir in macaroni, salt, herbs and lemon pepper. Microwave covered on low power (defrost) just until macaroni is tender, 12 to 14 minutes.

3. Stir in tuna and parsley. Cover evenly with Monterey Jack cheese; sprinkle with Parmesan cheese. Microwave covered on full power until cheese melts, 4 to 5 minutes.

Chili Basted Roasted Chicken

Makes 4 to 6 servings

1   whole frying chicken (about 3 1/2 pounds or 1600 g)
1   medium onion, thinly sliced, separated into rings
1   clove garlic, minced
1/2 cup (125 mL) catsup
2   tablespoons (30 mL) brown sugar
1   tablespoon (15 mL) cider vinegar
1   teaspoon (5 mL) chili powder
1   teaspoon (5 mL) Worcestershire sauce

Youngsters enjoy the barbecue-like flavors of this crimson chicken. You might accompany it with noodles or spaghetti, salad and hard rolls.

1. Soak top and bottom of 3 1/4-quart (3.25 L) clay cooker in water about 15 minutes; drain.

2. Rinse chicken and pat dry, reserving giblets for other use. Place chicken, breast side up, in cooker; surround with onion rings. Mix garlic, catsup, brown sugar, vinegar, chili powder and Worcestershire sauce; drizzle over chicken.

3. Place covered cooker in microwave oven. Microwave on full power, basting two or three times with sauce, until chicken is glazed and tender, 30 to 35 minutes.

4. Carve chicken; spoon onions and sauce over chicken.

Teriyaki Chicken Drumsticks

Makes 4 servings

12   medium chicken drumsticks
      (about 2 1/2 pounds or 1125 g)
1   small onion, thinly sliced,
      separated into rings
1/2   cup (125 mL) soy sauce
3   tablespoons (45 mL) brown
      sugar
1/2   teaspoon (2 mL) ground ginger
1   clove garlic, minced
2   tablespoons (30 mL) dry sherry

First marinated for several hours in mixture of soy sauce, ginger and sherry, the chicken cooks in just 25 minutes. This is a pleasant dish for a summer evening.

1. Place chicken in shallow glass baking dish. Cover with onion rings. Mix remaining ingredients; pour into baking dish. Refrigerate covered several hours or overnight.

2. Soak top and bottom of 3 1/4-quart (3.25 L) clay cooker in water about 15 minutes; drain.

3. Place chicken, onion rings and 1/4 cup (60 mL) of the marinade in cooker, arranging drumsticks with meatier parts toward ends of cooker. Reserve remaining marinade for other uses.

4. Place covered cooker in microwave oven. Microwave on full power, turning chicken once and basting with cooking liquid once or twice, until tender, about 25 minutes.

Lemon-Honey Chicken Quarters

Makes 4 servings

3   tablespoons (45 mL) flour
1   teaspoon (5 mL) garlic salt
1   teaspoon (5 mL) paprika
1/8   teaspoon (0.5 mL) white
      pepper
1   frying chicken (3 to 3 1/2 pounds
      or 1350 to 1600 g), cut into
      quarters
3   tablespoons (45 mL) honey
1   tablespoon (15 mL) lemon
      juice
1   tablespoon (15 mL) soy sauce
1/4   teaspoon (1 mL) ground ginger

It takes only about half an hour to cook this handsome chicken dish in a microwave oven, but its honey and lemon flavor is rich and deep. For even cooking, arrange the chicken so the leg quarters are at the ends of the clay cooker and the breast quarters in the center.

1. Soak top and bottom of 3 1/4-quart (3.25 L) clay cooker in water about 15 minutes; drain.

2. Mix flour, garlic salt, paprika and pepper; coat chicken quarters with flour mixture. Place chicken, skin sides down, in cooker.

3. Place covered cooker in microwave oven. Microwave on full power 15 minutes. Turn chicken quarters skin sides up.

4. Mix honey, lemon juice, soy sauce and ginger in a glass bowl. Microwave on full power until mixture bubbles, about 45 seconds. Pour over chicken.

5. Microwave covered on full power, basting once or twice with cooking liquid, until chicken is tender and juices run clear when thigh is pierced, about 15 minutes.

6. Spoon cooking liquid over chicken and serve.

Golden Glazed Cauliflower

Makes 6 servings

1   medium head cauliflower
      (about 1 1/2 pounds or 675 g)
1/2 cup (125 mL) mayonnaise
1   teaspoon (5 mL) Dijon-style
      mustard
1   green onion with top, thinly
      sliced
1/2 cup (125 mL) shredded
      Cheddar cheese

When cooking a whole cauliflower in a soaked clay cooker in the microwave oven, it is not necessary to add any water — the vegetable cooks perfectly in its own steam. The cheese topping gives a piquant finishing touch.

1. Soak top and bottom of 2-quart (2 L) clay cooker in water about 15 minutes; drain.

2. Remove leaves and core from cauliflower. Place rounded side up in cooker.

3. Place covered cooker in microwave oven. Microwave on full power until crisp-tender, 10 to 12 minutes. Combine mayonnaise, mustard and green onion; spread over cauliflower. Sprinkle with cheese.

4. Microwave, uncovered on full power until cheese melts, 1 1/2 to 2 minutes. Let stand covered 2 minutes.

5. Break cauliflower into flowerettes; spoon cheese sauce over each serving.

Middle-Eastern Lamb Stew

Makes 8 servings

3   pounds (1350 g) boneless lamb
      shoulder, cut into 1-inch
      (2.5 cm) cubes
2   tablespoons (30 mL) flour
2   teaspoons (10 mL) salt
1   teaspoon (5 mL) paprika
1/2 teaspoon (2 mL) ground
      coriander
1/8 teaspoon (0.5 mL) pepper
1   large onion, finely chopped
2   cloves garlic, minced
1   rib celery, finely chopped
1   medium green pepper, cut into
      thin slivers
1   large can (28 ounces or 800 g)
      tomatoes, coarsely chopped,
      liquid reserved
2   tablespoons (30 mL) tomato
      paste
1   package (9 ounces or 250 g)
      frozen green beans, thawed

This vegetable-laden lamb stew boasts an abundance of richly flavored sauce and combines appealingly with rice.

1. Soak top and bottom of 3 1/4-quart (3.25 L) clay cooker in water about 15 minutes; drain.

2. Coat lamb cubes with mixture of flour, salt, paprika, coriander and pepper. Place in cooker.

3. Place covered cooker in microwave oven. Microwave on full power 15 minutes; stir lamb cubes. Stir in remaining ingredients except beans. Microwave covered on medium-low power (simmer), stirring two or three times, until meat and vegetables are tender, 1 to 1 1/4 hours.

4. Stir in green beans. Microwave covered on medium-low power (simmer) just until beans are tender, 6 to 8 minutes.

Makes 6 servings

Custardy Baked Zucchini with Cheese

4   medium zucchini (about 1¼
     pounds or 550 g), unpared
1   teaspoon (5 mL) salt
1   tablespoon (15 mL) melted
     butter or margarine
4   eggs
1   clove garlic, minced
1   teaspoon (5 mL) Dijon-style
     mustard
¼   cup (60 mL) all-purpose flour
¼   teaspoon (1 mL) baking
     powder
⅛   teaspoon (0.5 mL) white
     pepper
⅛   teaspoon (0.5 mL) ground
     nutmeg
2   green onions with tops, thinly
     sliced
1   cup (250 mL) shredded Swiss
     cheese

Pretty and pale green, this zucchini casserole can be served either as a vegetable or a luncheon main dish — much as you might serve a vegetable and cheese omelet — with sliced tomatoes and flaky croissants.

1. Shred zucchini and spread on paper toweling. Sprinkle with salt. Let stand 1 hour.

2. Soak top and bottom of 3¼-quart (3.25 L) clay cooker in water about 15 minutes; drain.

3. Pat dry and brush bottom and sides of cooker with butter. Beat eggs, garlic, mustard, flour, baking powder, pepper and nutmeg until smooth. Stir in zucchini, green onions and cheese gently. Pour into cooker.

4. Place covered cooker in microwave oven. Microwave on full power, stirring once, until custard is set near center, about 15 minutes. Let stand covered about 3 minutes.

Makes 4 to 6 servings

Chicken Breasts with Creamy Mushroom Sauce

¼   pound (115 g) mushrooms,
     thinly sliced
2   green onions with tops, thinly
     sliced
3   whole chicken breasts (about 3
     pounds or 1350 g), boned,
     skinned, cut into halves
1   tablespoon (15 mL) flour
1   teaspoon (5 mL) salt
¼   teaspoon (1 mL) paprika
⅛   teaspoon (0.5 mL) white
     pepper
     Pinch nutmeg
¼   cup (60 mL) dry white wine
½   cup (125 mL) shredded aged
     Swiss cheese
½   cup (125 mL) whipping cream
     Thinly sliced green onions

This is an easy way to prepare chicken breasts, yet the finished dish is subtle and elegant enough for a special dinner. Accompany it with rice and asparagus spears.

1. Soak top and bottom of 3¼-quart (3.25 L) clay cooker in water about 15 minutes; drain.

2. Combine mushrooms and 2 green onions in cooker. Coat chicken breasts with mixture of flour, salt, paprika, pepper and nutmeg. Arrange chicken, slightly overlapping pieces on mushroom mixture. Pour in wine.

3. Place covered cooker in microwave oven. Microwave on full power until chicken is tender and juices run clear when chicken at center of cooker is pierced, 18 to 20 minutes. Remove chicken breasts to warm serving platter; keep warm.

4. Stir cheese and cream into liquid in cooker. Microwave uncovered on full power, stirring once or twice, until sauce bubbles and thickens slightly, about 7 minutes. Stir thoroughly; pour over chicken breasts. Garnish with green onions.

Makes 4 servings

Sweet and Sour Pork Chops

4   pork loin chops (2 pounds or 900 g), about 1 inch (2.5 cm) thick, fat trimmed
1   medium onion, thinly sliced, separated into rings
1   medium carrot, pared, cut diagonally into thin slices
1   small can (8 ounces or 225 g) unsweetened pineapple chunks, drained, liquid reserved
1   clove garlic, minced
1/3   cup (80 mL) packed brown sugar
1/3   cup (80 mL) red wine vinegar
1/4   cup (60 mL) catsup
1   tablespoon (15 mL) soy sauce
1   medium green pepper, cut into 1-inch (2.5 cm) squares
  Salt
2   teaspoons (10 mL) cornstarch

Pork chops will be tender and moist with a colorful mixture of carrots, green pepper and pineapple in a zesty sauce.

1. Soak top and bottom of 3 1/4-quart (3.25 L) clay cooker in water about 15 minutes; drain.

2. Place pork chops, slightly overlapping, in cooker. Cover with onion rings, carrot slices, pineapple chunks and garlic. Sprinkle with brown sugar. Mix vinegar, catsup and soy sauce; pour into cooker.

3. Place covered cooker in microwave oven. Microwave on full power 15 minutes. Add green pepper. Microwave covered on medium-low power (simmer) 20 minutes. Turn pork chops. Microwave covered until pork is completely cooked 8 to 10 minutes.

4. Remove pork chops to warm serving bowl. Sprinkle with salt. Remove pineapple and vegetables from cooking liquid with slotted spoon; spoon over pork chops.

5. Skim and discard fat from cooking liquid. Mix cornstarch and 1 tablespoon (15 mL) of the reserved pineapple liquid; stir into cooking liquid. Microwave uncovered on full power until sauce bubbles and thickens, about 3 minutes. Stir sauce and pour over pork chops.

Makes 6 servings

Green Pepper Beef

2   pounds (900 g) beef top round, cut into thin bite-size strips
1   tablespoon (15 mL) cornstarch
3/4   teaspoon (4 mL) salt
1/2   teaspoon (2 mL) ground ginger
1/2   teaspoon (2 mL) dry mustard
1/8   teaspoon (0.5 mL) seasoned pepper
1   medium onion, thinly sliced, separated into rings
1   clove garlic, minced
1   large green pepper, cut into thin strips
1   medium tomato, peeled, seeded, chopped
1/4   cup (60 mL) soy sauce

Here is a well browned, Chinese-style beef dish to serve with fluffy rice.

1. Soak top and bottom of 3 1/4-quart (3.25 L) clay cooker in water about 15 minutes; drain.

2. Coat beef strips with mixture of cornstarch, salt, ginger, mustard and pepper. Place in cooker.

3. Place covered cooker in microwave oven. Microwave on full power 10 minutes. Stir in remaining ingredients.

4. Microwave covered, on medium-low power (simmer), stirring once or twice, until beef is tender, about 45 minutes.

120

German Hot Potato Salad

Makes 6 servings

6 slices bacon, cut crosswise into 1/2-inch (1.5 cm) strips
4 medium boiling potatoes (about 2 pounds or 900 g), unpared
1 medium onion, finely chopped
1/3 cup (80 mL) white wine vinegar
1/3 cup (80 mL) regular-strength beef broth, canned or homemade
1 teaspoon (5 mL) salt
1/2 teaspoon (2 mL) sugar
Pinch white pepper
2 tablespoons (30 mL) minced fresh parsley

This hot potato salad is a lively companion to hot sausages or corned beef, with rye bread and beer.

1. Soak top and bottom of 3 1/4-quart (3.25 L) clay cooker in water about 15 minutes; drain.

2. Spread bacon strips in cooker.

3. Place covered cooker in microwave oven. Microwave on full power until bacon is brown, 10 to 12 minutes. Remove bacon with slotted spoon; reserve. Remove fat from cooker; reserve 2 tablespoons (30 mL) of the fat.

4. Pierce each potato in several places with fork; place in cooker. Microwave covered until tender, 15 to 20 minutes; remove potatoes from cooker. Add reserved bacon fat and the onions to cooker. Microwave covered on full power until tender, 3 to 4 minutes.

5. Slip skins off potatoes; cut into 1/2-inch (1.5 cm) cubes.

6. Add vinegar, broth, salt, sugar and pepper to onions. Microwave uncovered on full power until fully boiling, about 5 minutes.

7. Stir in potatoes. Microwave covered on full power until potatoes are hot, about 3 minutes. Stir in bacon and parsley gently. Serve hot.

Glazed Lamb Loaf

Makes 6 servings

1 egg
1/3 cup (80 mL) catsup
1 1/2 teaspoons (7 mL) salt
1/2 teaspoon (2 mL) dry mustard
1 clove garlic, minced
2 cups (500 mL) fresh bread crumbs
1 tart apple, pared, shredded
1/4 cup (60 mL) finely chopped green pepper
1 1/2 pounds (675 g) ground lamb
1/3 cup (80 mL) chutney

With tangy apples added to the ground lamb and a spicy chutney glaze, this meat loaf is a treat for lamb enthusiasts.

1. Soak top and bottom of 2-quart (2 L) clay cooker in water about 15 minutes; drain.

2. Beat egg in medium bowl; stir in catsup, salt, mustard and garlic. Stir in bread crumbs, apple and green pepper. Add lamb; mix well. Pat meat mixture into cooker. Process chutney in blender or food processor until smooth; brush over meat.

3. Place covered cooker in microwave oven. Microwave on full power until edges brown and juices run clear when knife is inserted in center, 20 to 25 minutes.

4. Let stand covered 5 minutes. Cut into slices.

Yams in Orange Sauce

Makes 4 to 6 servings

4   medium yams (about 2 pounds
     or 900 g), unpared
2   oranges
     Water
1/3 cup (80 mL) packed brown
     sugar
1/4 cup (60 mL) butter or
     margarine
1/4 teaspoon (1 mL) ground
     cinnamon
     Pinch ground nutmeg
2   teaspoons (10 mL) cornstarch
1   tablespoon (15 mL) water

Yams in luscious tart-sweet sauce taste good with roast pork or baked ham.

1. Soak top and bottom of 3 1/4-quart (3.25 L) clay cooker in water about 15 minutes; drain.

2. Pierce each yam in several places with fork. Place yams in cooker.

3. Place covered cooker in microwave oven. Microwave on full power just until yams are tender, 16 to 20 minutes. Remove yams from cooker. Let stand until cool enough to handle; slip off skins and cut lengthwise into quarters.

4. Grate enough orange rind to measure 2 teaspoons (10 mL). Squeeze juice from oranges; measure and add water, if needed, to make 1 cup (250 mL). Mix orange juice, orange rind, brown sugar, butter, cinnamon and nutmeg in cooker. Microwave uncovered on full power until fully boiling 6 to 8 minutes. Mix cornstarch and 1 tablespoon (15 mL) water; stir into cooker. Microwave covered on full power until thickened, about 3 minutes. Stir thoroughly. Stir in yams, turning to coat with sauce.

5. Microwave covered on full power until yams are hot, 3 to 5 minutes.

Lemony Lamb Shanks with Rice

Makes 4 servings

4   lamb shanks (3 to 3 1/2 pounds
      or 1350 to 1600 g)
2   tablespoons (30 mL) flour
2   teaspoons (10 mL) salt
1   teaspoon (5 mL) paprika
1   clove garlic, minced
1   bay leaf
1 1/2 cups (375 mL) regular-strength
      chicken broth, canned or
      homemade
1   lemon
1/2   cup (125 mL) uncooked long-
      grain white rice
2   tablespoons (30 mL) golden
      raisins

Cooking raisin-studded rice in the juices of lamb shanks enhances its flavor and produces a hearty dish; accompany with a lettuce-and-cucumber salad and crisp bread.

1. Soak top and bottom of 3 1/4-quart (3.25 L) clay cooker in water about 15 minutes; drain.

2. Coat lamb shanks with mixture of flour, salt and paprika. Place lamb shanks in cooker. Add garlic, bay leaf and chicken broth. Grate lemon rind; squeeze juice, add to cooker with lemon rind.

3. Place covered cooker in microwave oven. Microwave on full power 20 minutes; turn lamb shanks. Microwave covered on medium-low power (simmer) until lamb shanks are nearly tender, about 35 minutes.

4. Remove lamb shanks. Skim and discard fat from cooking liquid. Stir rice and raisins into cooking liquid. Microwave covered on full power until rice is tender, about 20 minutes. Arrange lamb shanks over rice in cooker. Microwave covered on medium-low power (simmer) until lamb is tender and hot, 5 to 10 minutes.

Breads with Brick-Oven Crustiness and Flavor

All over the world, the most prized breads are baked in brick ovens. The pueblo breads of the American Southwest, the pizza of Naples and the elegant whole grain loaves of the stylish bakery Poilane in Paris all have at least two things in common—incomparably crisp crusts and brick-oven baking.

A clay cooker makes it possible to achieve this combination in your own kitchen on a modest but versatile scale. You can use it to bake all kinds of breads: everyday white bread with extraordinary flavor, whole grain breads, French bread, sweet yeast breads and coffeecakes, and quick fruit and nut loaves.

For baking bread, choose a clay cooker of appropriate shape for the loaf. A small, loaf-shaped 5½-cup (1375 mL) clay cooker is perfect for many loaves, both yeast and quick breads. French bread bakes nicely in a long narrow clay cooker intended for fish.

Before baking bread, soak the clay cooker as you do for other uses. The steamy interior is one of the secrets of crisp crusts. Yeast breads rise in the soaked lower portion of the clay cooker, then, just before baking, are covered with the soaked lid.

If a bread comes close to filling the covered clay cooker, you can expect it to brown beautifully with the cover in place. However, if, at the time a bread tests done, it is not brown enough to satisfy you, uncover it and let it bake at the same oven temperature for another 2 to 5 minutes.

To prevent bread from sticking, grease the clay cooker well before placing the dough in it. High-rising yeast breads make it advisable to grease the inside of the cover, as well. Use a soft, all-purpose vegetable shortening. To facilitate removing bread from the clay cooker, line the cooker with baking parchment paper cut to fit the bottom when you bake sweet yeast breads, quick breads (tender and delicate when hot), and any bread with a sticky filling or topping.

With all these suggestions in mind, you are now ready for one of the most satisfying experiences an enthusiastic baker can derive from a clay cooker—baking bread!

One Perfect Loaf

1   **cup (250 mL) warm water (105° to 115°F or 40° to 45°C)**
1   **package active dry yeast**
1   **teaspoon (5 mL) sugar**
3/4   **teaspoon (4 mL) salt**
1   **tablespoon (15 mL) vegetable oil**
3   **cups (750 mL) all-purpose flour (approximately)**

Baking bread in a wet clay cooker results in a crisp shiny crust you may have thought possible only in a baker's brick oven. If you have doubts, try this simple single loaf.

1. Place warm water in large mixer bowl; sprinkle with yeast. Let stand until softened, about 3 minutes. Stir in sugar, salt and oil. Add 2 cups (500 mL) of the flour. Mix until blended; beat on medium speed until dough is elastic and pulls away from bowl, about 5 minutes.

2. Stir in 1/2 cup (125 mL) of the flour to make soft dough. Turn dough onto floured surface. Knead, adding flour as needed, until dough is smooth and springy and small bubbles form just under surface, 15 to 20 minutes.

3. Place dough in greased bowl; turn greased side up. Let stand covered in warm place until doubled, about 1 hour.

4. Soak bottom of loaf-shaped, 51/2-cup (1375 mL) clay cooker in water about 15 minutes. When dough has doubled, drain bottom of cooker; pat dry; grease sides and bottom generously.

5. Punch down dough; shape into loaf and place in cooker. Let stand, covered with waxed paper, in warm place until dough nearly reaches top of cooker, 30 to 45 minutes. Cut diagonal slashes, 1/2 inch (1.5 cm) deep, in top of dough with razor blade or sharp knife.

6. Soak top of cooker in water about 15 minutes; drain; pat dry and grease. Place covered cooker in cold oven. Set oven at 475°F (250°C). Bake 45 minutes. Remove cover; bake until top is brown, 3 to 5 minutes. Remove from cooker; cool on wire rack.

To Bake Frozen Bread Dough

2   **tablespoons (30 mL) melted butter or margarine**
1   **loaf frozen bread dough (1 pound or 450 g)**

Purists may scoff, but for an easy way to experience the potential of clay cooker bread baking, why not try a loaf of frozen bread dough. It rises high and wide, and the crust is the best it can be.

1. Brush sides and bottom of loaf-shaped, 51/2-cup (1375 mL) clay cooker with half the butter. Place frozen dough, bottom side up, in cooker. Brush dough with remaining butter.

2. Refrigerate overnight or let stand in warm place 1 to 2 hours to thaw.

3. Let stand, covered with waxed paper, in warm place until dough rises nearly to top of cooker, 1 to 3 hours.

TO BAKE FROZEN DOUGH BREAD, continued

4. Soak top of cooker in water about 15 minutes; drain.

5. Place covered cooker in cold oven. Set oven at 450°F (230°C). Bake until brown, 40 to 45 minutes. Remove from cooker; cool on wire rack.

Braided Egg Bread

Makes 1 loaf

1/2 cup (125 mL) milk
6   tablespoons (90 mL) butter or margarine
2   tablespoons (30 mL) sugar
1/2 teaspoon (2 mL) salt
1/4 cup (60 mL) warm water (105° to 115°F or 40° to 45°C)
1   package active dry yeast
3 1/2 cups (875 mL) all-purpose flour (approximately)
3   eggs
1   egg white
1   teaspoon (5 mL) water
1   teaspoon (5 mL) sesame seeds

This lovely plump loaf can be baked in the all-purpose 3 1/4-quart (3.25 L) clay cooker. The sesame seeded crust is crisp, yet tender.

1. Scald milk; remove from heat. Stir in butter, sugar and salt, stirring until butter melts. Pour into large mixer bowl; cool to lukewarm. Place 1/4 cup (60 mL) warm water in small bowl; sprinkle with yeast. Let stand until softened, about 3 minutes.

2. Add yeast mixture and 1 3/4 cups (430 mL) of the flour to milk mixture. Mix until blended; beat on medium speed until dough is elastic and pulls away from bowl, about 5 minutes.

3. Beat in whole eggs, one at a time, beating well after each addition. Beat in 1 cup (250 mL) of the flour. Stir in 1/2 cup (125 mL) of the flour to make soft dough. Turn dough onto floured surface. Knead, adding flour as needed, until dough is smooth and satiny and small bubbles form just under surface, about 15 minutes.

4. Place dough in greased bowl; turn greased side up. Let stand covered in warm place until doubled, about 1 1/2 hours.

5. Soak bottom of a 3 1/4-quart (3.25 L) clay cooker in water about 15 minutes. When dough has doubled, drain bottom of cooker; pat dry; grease sides and bottom generously. Line cooker with parchment paper cut to fit bottom only; grease parchment paper.

6. Punch down dough. Turn onto floured surface. Knead lightly just to expel air bubbles. Divide into 3 pieces. Roll each piece between palms of hands into 12-inch (30 cm) rope. Place ropes, side by side, in cooker; braid ropes and tuck ends under. Let stand, covered with waxed paper, in warm place until nearly doubled, 45 minutes to 1 hour. Mix egg white and 1 teaspoon (5 mL) water. Brush dough with egg white mixture; sprinkle with sesame seeds.

7. Soak top of cooker in water about 15 minutes; drain. Place covered cooker in cold oven. Set oven at 425°F (220°C). Bake until bread sounds hollow when tapped and crust is brown, 40 to 45 minutes. Remove from cooker; cool on wire rack.

Makes 1 large coffeecake

Lemon Pull-Apart Loaf

1	**cup (250 mL) milk**
6	**tablespoons (90 mL) butter or margarine**
¹/₂	**cup (125 mL) sugar**
1	**teaspoon (5 mL) salt**
¹/₂	**cup (125 mL) warm water (105° to 115°F or 40° to 45°C)**
3	**packages active dry yeast**
5¹/₂	**cups (1375 mL) all-purpose flour (approximately)**
2	**eggs**
	Lemon Sugar (recipe follows)
	Lemon Glaze (recipe follows)

Bake balls of lemon-sugared, sweet yeast dough in the versatile 3¹/₄-quart (3.25 L) clay cooker to make a caramel-crusted loaf that is drizzled with a lemon glaze. It can be sliced as a loaf if you wish, but it's more fun to pull the easily defined spheres of dough apart.

1. Scald milk; remove from heat. Stir in 4 tablespoons (60 mL) of the butter, the sugar and salt, stirring until butter melts. Pour into large mixer bowl; cool to lukewarm. Place warm water in small bowl; sprinkle with yeast. Let stand until softened, about 3 minutes.

2. Add yeast mixture and 3 cups (750 mL) of the flour to milk mixture. Mix until blended; beat on medium speed until dough is elastic and pulls away from bowl, about 5 minutes.

3. Beat in eggs, one at a time, beating well after each addition. Beat in 1 cup (250 mL) of the flour. Stir in 1 cup (250 mL) of the flour to make soft dough. Turn dough onto floured surface. Knead, adding flour as needed, until dough is smooth and satiny and small bubbles form under surface, 15 to 20 minutes.

4. Place dough in greased bowl; turn greased side up. Let stand covered in warm place until doubled, about 45 minutes.

5. Soak bottom of 3¹/₄-quart (3.25 L) clay cooker in water about 15 minutes. When dough has doubled, drain bottom of cooker; pat dry; grease sides and bottom generously. Line cooker with parchment paper cut to fit bottom only; grease parchment paper.

6. Make Lemon Sugar

7. Punch down dough. Turn onto floured surface. Knead lightly just to expel air bubbles. Cut dough in half; divide each half into 16 pieces. Roll each piece into ball, tucking ends under. Place 16 balls in cooker.

8. Melt remaining butter. Brush dough in cooker with half the melted butter. Sprinkle with half the Lemon Sugar. Cover with remaining 16 balls of dough. Brush with remaining butter; sprinkle with remaining Lemon Sugar.

9. Let stand, covered with waxed paper, in warm place until dough nearly reaches top of clay cooker, 35 to 45 minutes.

10. Soak top of cooker in water about 15 minutes; drain. Place covered cooker in cold oven. Set oven at 400°F (200°C). Bake until bread sounds hollow when tapped and crust is brown, about 45 minutes.

11. Make Lemon Glaze.

12. Let cooker stand 5 minutes; carefully invert onto wire rack. Drizzle with Lemon Glaze. Serve warm or at room temperature.

(Continued on page 130)

LEMON PULL-APART LOAF, continued

Lemon Sugar

1/2   cup (125 mL) sugar
1/4   teaspoon (1 mL) ground mace
        or nutmeg
        Grated rind of 2 lemons

1. Mix all ingredients in small bowl.

Lemon Glaze

1   cup (250 mL) powdered sugar
1   teaspoon (5 mL) butter or
        margarine, room
        temperature
2   tablespoons (30 mL) lemon
        juice

1. Mix all ingredients in medium bowl until smooth.

Cherry Almond Ribbon Coffeecake

Makes 1 coffeecake

1   cup (250 mL) milk
1/4   cup (60 mL) butter or
        margarine
1/2   cup (125 mL) sugar
1   teaspoon (5 mL) salt
1/4   cup (60 mL) warm water (105°
        to 115°F or 40° to 45°C)
2   packages active dry yeast
5   cups (1250 mL) all-purpose
        flour (approximately)
1   teaspoon (5 mL) vanilla
2   eggs
        Almond Filling (recipe
        follows)
1/2   cup (125 mL) chopped candied
        red cherries
        Powdered Sugar Glaze (recipe
        follows)
        Sliced toasted almonds

A festive choice for a big family breakfast or brunch, this recipe produces a spectacular long loaf in a clay cooker designed for fish.

1. Scald milk in small saucepan; remove from heat. Stir in butter, sugar and salt, stirring until butter melts. Pour into large mixer bowl; cool to lukewarm. Place warm water in small bowl; sprinkle with yeast. Let stand until softened, about 3 minutes.

2. Add yeast mixture and 2 1/2 cups (625 mL) of the flour to milk mixture. Mix until blended; beat on medium speed until dough is elastic and pulls away from bowl, about 5 minutes.

3. Beat in vanilla and eggs, one at a time, beating well after each addition. Beat in 1 cup (250 mL) of the flour. Stir in 1 cup (250 mL) of the flour to make soft dough. Turn dough onto floured surface. Knead, adding flour as needed, until dough is smooth and satiny and small bubbles form just under surface, 15 to 20 minutes.

4. Place dough in greased bowl; turn greased side up. Let stand covered in warm place until doubled, 1 1/4 to 1 1/2 hours.

5. Soak bottom of long 2 3/4-quart (2.75 L) clay cooker about 15 minutes. When dough has doubled, drain bottom of cooker; pat dry; grease sides and bottom generously. Line cooker with parchment paper cut to fit bottom only; grease parchment paper.

(Continued on page 132)

CHERRY ALMOND RIBBON CAKE, continued

6. While dough is rising, make Almond Filling.

7. Punch down dough. Turn onto floured surface; knead lightly just to expel air bubbles. Cover dough with inverted bowl; let stand 10 minutes. Roll out dough into 15-inch (38 cm) square. Spread Almond Filling with spatula over dough. Sprinkle cherries over filling. Fold dough in thirds, making 15x5-inch (38x13 cm) strip. Cut dough into 12 equal slices. Arrange slices, cut sides up, in cooker.

8. Let stand, covered with waxed paper, in warm place until dough nearly reaches top of clay cooker, about 45 minutes.

9. Soak top of cooker in water about 15 minutes; drain. Place covered cooker in cold oven. Set oven at 400°F (200°C). Bake until brown and wooden pick inserted in center comes out clean, 45 to 55 minutes.

10. Make Powdered Sugar Glaze.

11. Let cooker stand 5 minutes. Remove bread from cooker; cool on wire rack. Drizzle Powdered Sugar Glaze over warm coffeecake; sprinkle with almonds. Serve warm or at room temperature.

Almond Filling

3/4 cup (180 mL) ground unblanched almonds
1/3 cup (80 mL) sugar
1/4 cup (60 mL) fine dry bread crumbs
2 tablespoons (30 mL) melted butter or margarine
1/4 teaspoon (1 mL) almond extract
1 egg

1. Combine almonds, sugar and bread crumbs in medium bowl. Stir in butter and almond extract. Add egg; mix well.

Powdered Sugar Glaze

---

1 cup (250 mL) powdered sugar
4 teaspoons (20 mL) warm water
1 teaspoon (5 mL) butter, room temperature
   Dash vanilla

1. Mix all ingredients in medium bowl until smooth.

Makes 1 loaf

Date Orange Bread

2   eggs
1   cup (250 mL) packed brown
**   sugar**
3   tablespoons (45 mL) vegetable
**   oil**
1   tablespoon (15 mL) grated
**   orange rind**
1   teaspoon (5 mL) vanilla
2¹/₂ cups (625 mL) all-purpose
**   flour**
1   teaspoon (5 mL) salt
1   teaspoon (5 mL) baking soda
2   teaspoons (10 mL) baking
**   powder**
³/₄ cup (180 mL) orange juice
1¹/₂ cups (375 mL) finely chopped
**   pitted dates**

Fresh orange juice and rind give this moist, crisp crusted date bread a luscious taste. It slices well, even when it is slightly warm. Try it for tea sandwiches with fluffy cream cheese.

1. Soak top and bottom of loaf-shaped, 5¹/₂-cup (1375 mL) clay cooker in water about 15 minutes; drain. Pat dry and generously grease inside surfaces of bottom of cooker. Line cooker with parchment paper cut to fit bottom only; grease parchment paper.

2. Beat eggs and brown sugar in large mixer bowl until light and creamy. Beat in oil, orange rind and vanilla.

3. Mix flour, salt, baking soda and baking powder. Add half of flour mixture to egg mixture; mix just until blended. Add half of orange juice to egg mixture; mix just until blended. Repeat with remaining flour and orange juice. Fold in dates. Spread batter in cooker.

4. Place covered cooker in cold oven. Set oven at 400°F (200°C). Bake until wooden pick inserted in center comes out clean, 45 to 50 minutes.

5. Let cooker stand on wire rack 10 minutes. Remove bread from cooker; cool on rack. Cut into thin slices.

Makes 1 loaf

Cinnamon Coffee Bread

¹/₄ cup (60 mL) butter, room
**   temperature**
¹/₂ cup (125 mL) sugar
1   egg
¹/₂ teaspoon (2 mL) vanilla
1¹/₂ cups (375 mL) all-purpose
**   flour**
2   teaspoons (10 mL) baking
**   powder**
¹/₄ teaspoon (1 mL) salt
¹/₃ cup (80 mL) fresh, strong
**   coffee**
¹/₃ cup (80 mL) half-and-half
¹/₄ cup (60 mL) sugar
1   teaspoon (5 mL) ground
**   cinnamon**

The generous cinnamon-sugar sprinkling of this moist, fine-textured quick bread forms a crispy fragile crust.

1. Soak top and bottom of loaf-shaped, 5¹/₂-cup (1375 mL) clay cooker in water about 15 minutes; drain. Pat dry and generously grease bottom and sides of cooker. Line cooker with parchment paper cut to fit bottom only; grease parchment paper.

2. Cream butter and ¹/₂ cup (125 mL) sugar in large mixer bowl until fluffy. Beat in egg and vanilla. Mix flour, baking powder and salt. Add half the flour mixture to butter mixture; beat until smooth. Mix in coffee. Beat in remaining flour mixture. Add half-and-half; beat until smooth. Spread batter in cooker.

3. Mix ¹/₄ cup (60 mL) sugar and the cinnamon. Sprinkle evenly over batter.

4. Place covered cooker in cold oven. Set oven at 400°F (200°C). Bake until wooden pick inserted in center comes out clean, 40 to 50 minutes.

5. Let cooker stand on wire rack about 10 minutes. Remove bread from cooker; cool on rack. Serve thick slices warm or at room temperature.

Molasses Bran Brown Bread

Makes 1 loaf

1 egg
1 cup (250 mL) whole-bran cereal
1/2 cup (125 mL) dark raisins
3/4 cup (180 mL) water
1/3 cup (80 mL) light molasses
2 tablespoons (30 mL) vegetable oil
1 cup (250 mL) all-purpose flour
1 teaspoon (5 mL) baking soda
1/2 teaspoon (2 mL) salt
1/2 teaspoon (2 mL) ground cinnamon

Baked rather than steamed, this brown bread will remind you of the classic Boston kind. It is good with Mrs. B's Baked Beans (see Index for page number).

1. Soak top and bottom of loaf-shaped, 5 1/2-cup (1375 mL) clay cooker in water about 15 minutes; drain. Pat dry and generously grease inside surfaces of bottom of cooker. Line cooker with parchment paper cut to fit bottom only; grease parchment paper.

2. Beat egg lightly in large mixer bowl. Mix in bran cereal, raisins, water, molasses and oil. Mix flour, baking soda, salt and cinnamon; stir into bran mixture just until blended. Spread batter in cooker.

3. Place covered cooker in cold oven. Set oven at 375°F (190°C). Bake until wooden pick inserted in center comes out clean, 45 to 55 minutes.

4. Transfer bread to board; slice and serve warm.

Cheese Puff Bread

Makes 8 servings

1 cup (250 mL) milk
1/4 cup (60 mL) butter or margarine
1/2 teaspoon (2 mL) salt
    Pinch ground nutmeg
1 cup (250 mL) all-purpose flour
4 eggs
1 cup (250 mL) shredded Swiss cheese

This bread (called gougère) begins with a cream puff dough, but the addition of shredded Swiss cheese and clay-cooker baking turn it into a savory and crusty creation. It is especially nice for a supper with soup or a seafood salad.

1. Soak top and bottom of 3 1/4-quart (3.25 L) clay cooker in water about 15 minutes; drain. Pat dry and grease inside surfaces of bottom of cooker. Line cooker with parchment paper cut to fit bottom only; grease parchment paper.

2. Place milk, butter, salt and nutmeg in a 2-quart (2 L) saucepan. Heat to boiling; add flour all at once. Cook and stir over medium heat until mixture pulls away from sides of pan and forms a ball, about 2 minutes; remove from heat.

3. Beat in eggs, one at a time, by hand, until mixture is smooth. Beat in half of the cheese.

4. Divide mixture into 8 portions. Using 2 spoons, shape each portion into rounded mound in cooker, placing 3 mounds along each side and 1 at each end. Sprinkle with remaining cheese.

5. Place covered cooker in cold oven. Set oven at 400°F (200°C). Bake until puffs are brown and crisp, about 1 1/4 hours.

6. Divide puffs and serve immediately.

Liz' Honey Whole Wheat Bread

Makes 1 loaf

2   cups (500 mL) whole wheat
      flour
1/4   cup (60 mL) nonfat dry
      milk
1 1/2   teaspoons (7 mL) salt
1   package active dry yeast
1 1/4   cups (310 mL) warm water
      (105° to 115°F or 40° to
      45°C)
1/4   cup (60 mL) honey
1   tablespoon (15 mL) vegetable
      oil
2   cups (500 mL) all-purpose
      flour (approximately)

With a dense, sweetly nutlike flavor, this bread makes healthy sandwiches and marvelous toast.

1. Combine whole wheat flour, dry milk, salt and yeast in large mixer bowl. Add warm water, honey and oil. Mix until blended; beat on medium speed 3 minutes.

2. Stir in 1 1/2 cups (375 mL) of the all-purpose flour to make stiff dough. Turn dough onto floured surface. Knead, adding flour as needed, until dough is smooth and elastic and small bubbles form just under surface, 15 to 20 minutes.

3. Place dough in greased bowl; turn greased side up. Let stand covered in warm place until doubled, about 1 1/4 to 1 1/2 hours.

4. Soak top and bottom of a loaf-shaped, 5 1/2-cup (1375 mL) clay cooker in water about 15 minutes. When dough has doubled, drain bottom of cooker; pat dry; grease sides and bottom generously.

5. Punch down dough; shape into oblong loaf and place in cooker. Let stand, covered with waxed paper, in warm place until dough nearly reaches top of cooker, 25 to 30 minutes.

6. Drain top of cooker; pat dry and grease. Place covered cooker in cold oven. Set oven at 425°F (220°C). Bake until bread sounds hollow when tapped, 40 to 45 minutes. Remove cover; bake until top is dark brown, 2 to 4 minutes. Remove from cooker; cool on wire rack.

French Bread

Makes 1 loaf

1 1/3   cups (330 mL) warm water
      (105° to 115°F or 40° to
      45°C)
1   package active dry yeast
1   tablespoon (15 mL) sugar
2   teaspoons (10 mL) salt
1   tablespoon (15 mL) vegetable
      oil
4   cups (1 L) all-purpose flour
      (approximately)

Here is a long crusty loaf, baked in an elongated clay cooker designed for fish.

1. Place warm water in large mixer bowl; sprinkle with yeast. Let stand until softened, about 3 minutes. Stir in sugar, salt and oil. Add 2 3/4 cups (680 mL) of the flour. Mix until blended; beat on medium speed until dough is elastic and pulls away from bowl, about 5 minutes.

2. Stir in 3/4 cup (180 mL) of the flour to make soft dough. Turn dough onto floured surface. Knead, adding flour as needed, until dough is smooth and springy and small bubbles form just under surface, 20 to 25 minutes.

FRENCH BREAD, continued

3. Place dough in greased bowl; turn greased side up. Let stand covered in warm place until doubled, 1 to 1 1/2 hours.

4. Soak bottom of long 2 3/4-quart (2.75 L) clay cooker in water about 15 minutes. When dough has doubled, drain bottom of cooker; pat dry; grease sides and bottom generously.

5. Punch down dough; shape into narrow loaf, about 11 inches (28 cm) long, and place in cooker. Let stand, covered with waxed paper, in warm place until nearly doubled, about 45 minutes. Cut 3 diagonal slashes, 1 inch (2.5 cm) deep, in top of dough with razor blade or sharp knife.

6. Soak top of cooker in water about 15 minutes; drain. Place covered cooker in cold oven. Set oven at 475°F (250°C). Bake until bread sounds hollow when tapped, 45 to 50 minutes. Remove cover; bake until top is brown, 1 to 3 minutes. Remove from cooker; cool on wire rack.

Cranberry Raisin Spirals

Makes 12 rolls

2 cups (500 mL) all-purpose flour
1 tablespoon (15 mL) baking powder
1 teaspoon (5 mL) salt
3/4 cup (180 mL) butter or margarine
3/4 cup (180 mL) milk
2 tablespoons (30 mL) granulated sugar
1/2 cup (125 mL) fresh cranberries, cut into halves
1/4 cup (60 mL) dark raisins
Water
1/2 cup (125 mL) packed light brown sugar

Made from a biscuit dough, these fruit-filled rolls are both festive and quick to put together.

1. Soak top and bottom of 3 1/4-quart (3.25 L) clay cooker in water about 15 minutes; drain. Line cooker with parchment paper cut to fit bottom only.

2. Mix flour, baking powder and salt in medium bowl. Cut in 1/4 cup (60 mL) of the butter until mixture forms coarse crumbs; melt remaining 1/2 cup (125 mL) butter.

3. Stir milk into flour mixture to make soft dough. Turn out on floured surface; knead gently 30 seconds. Roll dough into 13x8-inch (33x20 cm) rectangle. Brush with 2 tablespoons (30 mL) of the melted butter, leaving 1/2-inch (1.5 cm) border on one long edge. Sprinkle with granulated sugar. Sprinkle dough with 6 tablespoons (90 mL) cranberries and the raisins. Roll up, beginning at long edge opposite border. Brush border with water and seal. Cut into 12 slices.

4. Pour remaining melted butter into cooker; brush butter about 3 inches (8 cm) up sides. Sprinkle with brown sugar and remaining cranberries. Arrange rolls in cooker in 2 rows of 6 slices each.

5. Place covered cooker in cold oven. Set oven at 475°F (250°C). Bake until rolls are light brown in center, 35 to 40 minutes.

6. Let cooker stand until mixture stops bubbling, about 3 minutes; carefully invert onto serving plate. Serve warm.

Strawberry Ripple Coffeecake

Makes 1 coffeecake, 8 servings

$^2/_3$ cup (160 mL) butter or margarine, room temperature
$^2/_3$ cup (160 mL) sugar
2 cups (500 mL) all-purpose flour
2 teaspoons (10 mL) baking powder
$^1/_2$ teaspoon (2 mL) salt
$^1/_2$ teaspoon (2 mL) baking soda
$^1/_2$ teaspoon (2 mL) ground cinnamon
$^1/_4$ teaspoon (1 mL) ground nutmeg
2 eggs
$^2/_3$ cup (160 mL) buttermilk
$^1/_3$ cup (80 mL) strawberry jam

Here is a tender, velvety spiced crumb cake with a sweet marbling of strawberries. Serve it warm for a special weekend breakfast.

1. Soak top and bottom of 3$^1/_4$-quart (3.25 L) clay cooker in water about 15 minutes; drain. Pat dry and grease inside surfaces of bottom of cooker. Line cooker with parchment paper cut to fit bottom only; grease parchment paper.

2. Cream butter and sugar in large mixer bowl until fluffy. Add $^3/_4$ cup (180 mL) of the flour; mix slowly just until mixture forms coarse crumbs. Remove and reserve $^2/_3$ cup (160 mL) of the crumb mixture.

3. Add baking powder, salt, baking soda, cinnamon, nutmeg and eggs to remaining mixture in mixer bowl; beat until smooth. Beat in remaining 1$^1/_4$ cups (310 mL) flour alternately with buttermilk, beating until smooth after each addition. Spread batter in cooker.

4. Drop jam by teaspoons over batter; cut jam into batter with knife to give marbled effect. Crumble reserved crumb mixture over top.

5. Place covered cooker in cold oven. Set oven at 400°F (200°C). Bake until brown and wooden pick inserted in center comes out clean, 40 to 45 minutes.

6. Cut into squares and serve warm.

Carrot Flecked Cornbread

Makes 8 servings

$^1/_4$ cup (60 mL) butter or margarine, melted
4 medium carrots, pared
2 cups (500 mL) buttermilk
2 eggs
2 cups (500 mL) yellow cornmeal
1 teaspoon (5 mL) salt
1 teaspoon (5 mL) baking powder
1 teaspoon (5 mL) baking soda
Butter

Speckled with colorful bits of carrot, this traditional cornbread served hot makes an ordinary family supper into a special occasion.

1. Soak top and bottom of 3$^1/_4$-quart (3.25 L) clay cooker in water about 15 minutes; drain. Pat bottom of cooker dry and brush with about 1 tablespoon (15 mL) of the melted butter. Line cooker with parchment paper cut to fit bottom only; butter parchment paper lightly.

2. Shred carrots in blender or food processor. Add buttermilk and eggs, process until mixed.

3. Mix cornmeal, salt, baking powder and soda. Add cornmeal mixture and remaining melted butter to carrot mixture; stir until blended. Pour batter into cooker.

4. Place covered cooker in cold oven. Set oven at 450°F (230°C). Bake until wooden pick inserted in center comes out clean and bread pulls away from cooker, about 30 minutes. Remove cover; bake until light brown, about 3 minutes. Serve warm with butter.

Makes 1 loaf

Elegant Almond Bread

1/2	cup (125 mL) butter or margarine, room temperature
1	cup (250 mL) sugar
1	egg
1/4	teaspoon (1 mL) almond extract
2	cups (500 mL) all-purpose flour
1/4	teaspoon (1 mL) baking powder
1/4	teaspoon (1 mL) baking soda
1/4	teaspoon (1 mL) salt
1/2	cup (125 mL) half-and-half
1/2	cup (125 mL) toasted slivered almonds*

Rich, delicate and cakelike, thin slices of this bread might be served with tea, in place of pound cake.

1. Soak top and bottom of loaf-shaped, 5 1/2-cup (1375 mL) clay cooker in water about 15 minutes; drain. Pat dry and generously grease inside surfaces of bottom of cooker. Line cooker with parchment paper cut to fit bottom only; grease parchment paper.

2. Cream butter and sugar in large mixer bowl until light and fluffy. Mix in egg and almond extract until blended.

3. Mix flour, baking powder, baking soda and salt. Add half of flour mixture to egg mixture; mix just until blended. Add 1/4 cup (60 mL) half-and-half to egg mixture, mix just until blended. Repeat with remaining flour and half-and-half. Fold in almonds; spread batter in cooker.

4. Place covered cooker in cold oven. Set oven at 375° (190°C). Bake until wooden pick inserted in center of bread comes out clean, about 1 hour and 5 minutes. Let cooker stand on wire rack 10 minutes. Remove bread from cooker; cool on rack. Cut into thin slices.

NOTE: *To toast almonds, spread in shallow pan and bake in 350°F (180°C) oven until light brown, 6 to 8 minutes.

Makes 1 loaf

Wheaty Zucchini Bread

2	eggs
1/2	cup (125 mL) vegetable oil
1/2	cup (125 mL) granulated sugar
1/2	cup (125 mL) packed brown sugar
1 1/2	teaspoons (7 mL) vanilla
1	cup (250 mL) coarsely shredded, unpared zucchini
1 1/2	cups (375 mL) all-purpose flour
1/4	cup (60 mL) graham flour
1	teaspoon (5 mL) baking soda
1	teaspoon (5 mL) salt
1/4	teaspoon (1 mL) baking powder
1/2	cup (125 mL) finely chopped walnuts

It's easy to taste the reason for the popularity of zucchini bread, especially when it is baked in a clay cooker to increase the crisp tenderness of the crust.

1. Soak top and bottom of loaf-shaped, 5 1/2-cup (1375 mL) clay cooker in water about 15 minutes; drain. Pat dry and grease inside surfaces of bottom of cooker. Line cooker with parchment paper cut to fit bottom only; grease parchment paper.

2. Beat eggs in large mixer bowl until blended. Add oil, sugars and vanilla; beat until thick and light. Stir in zucchini. Mix flours, baking soda, salt and baking powder; add to zucchini mixture and mix just until blended. Fold in walnuts. Spread batter in cooker.

3. Place covered cooker in cold oven. Set oven at 400°F (200°C). Bake until wooden pick inserted in center comes out clean, 55 minutes to 1 hour.

4. Let cooker stand on wire rack 10 minutes. Remove bread from cooker; cool on rack. Cut into thin slices.

Makes 1 loaf

Luscious Cinnamon Loaf

1/3	cup (80 mL) milk
2	tablespoons (30 mL) butter or margarine
6	tablespoons (90 mL) granulated sugar
1/2	teaspoon (2 mL) salt
1/4	cup (60 mL) warm water (105° to 115°F or 40° to 45°C)
1	package active dry yeast
2 1/2	cups (625 mL) all-purpose flour (approximately)
1 1/2	teaspoons (7 mL) grated lemon rind
1 1/2	teaspoons (7 mL) ground cinnamon
1	egg
	Powdered sugar

This sweet beige loaf is a splendid breakfast bread. Its flavor is a perfumed fragrance combining lemon and cinnamon — a combination that suggests its Portuguese origin. Because the dough is so rich and sweet, it rises rather slowly, both before and after shaping. When you make it, allow plenty of time. The bread is good warm with slivers of cold butter.

1. Scald milk in small saucepan; remove from heat. Stir in butter, granulated sugar and salt, stirring until butter melts. Pour into large mixer bowl; cool to lukewarm. Place warm water in small bowl; sprinkle with yeast. Let stand until softened, about 3 minutes.

2. Add yeast mixture and 1 1/4 cups (310 mL) of the flour to milk mixture. Mix until blended; beat on medium speed until dough is elastic and pulls away from bowl, about 3 minutes.

3. Beat in lemon rind, cinnamon and egg; beat until blended. Beat in 1/2 cup (125 mL) of the flour. Stir in 1/2 cup (125 mL) of the flour to make soft dough. Turn dough onto floured surface. Knead, adding flour as needed, until dough is smooth and satiny and small bubbles form just under surface, about 15 minutes.

4. Place dough in greased bowl; turn greased side up. Let stand covered in warm place until doubled, 2 1/2 to 3 hours.

5. Soak bottom of loaf-shaped, 5 1/2-cup (1375 mL) clay cooker in water about 15 minutes. When dough has doubled, drain bottom of cooker; pat dry; grease sides and bottom generously. Line cooker with parchment paper cut to fit bottom only; grease parchment paper.

6. Punch down dough. Turn onto floured surface; knead lightly just to expel air bubbles. Shape into oblong loaf and place in cooker.

7. Let stand, covered with waxed paper, in warm place until dough nearly reaches top of cooker, about 1 1/2 hours. Sift powdered sugar lightly over dough.

8. Soak top of cooker in water about 15 minutes; drain, pat dry and grease. Place covered cooker in cold oven. Set oven at 375°F (190°C). Bake until bread sounds hollow when tapped and crust is brown, about 45 minutes.

9. Let cooker stand 5 minutes. Remove bread from cooker; cool on wire rack. Sift powdered sugar generously over warm loaf. Serve warm or at room temperature.

Desserts to Serve Temptingly Warm

The perfect finish to a meal made in a clay cooker is a clay cooker dessert, served warm from the oven. The wonderful flavor clay cooking brings to meats, fish, poultry and vegetables is also irresistible when you crave something sweet.

What sort of desserts can you prepare in a clay cooker? The variety is amazing—baked fruits such as apples and pears, cobbler-type fruit puddings, old-fashioned rice pudding cooked in rich milk with plenty of raisins, delicate hot fruit soufflés, even deep-dish pies and delicious loaf cakes.

Many of these desserts are best when served warm from the oven. Plan to bake them along with a main dish or vegetables also prepared in a clay cooker to make the best use of oven heat. It is worthwhile having a second clay cooker for desserts. A 2- quart (2 L) cooker, either oblong or square, is a useful size.

Most desserts can be baked in the clay cooker without a paper liner. An exception is cakes. A tender cake will be easier to remove from the clay cooker with greased parchment paper lining the bottom.

Unlike many other foods, desserts can be baked in clay at approximately the same temperature you would use if baking them in any other container. Two kinds of desserts that definitely need a fairly gentle oven temperature when baked in clay are cakes and custards. If you use too high a baking temperature for a cake, it may become overbrown at the edges and corners before the center is completely baked. Custards and puddings thickened with eggs may separate and weep at too high a temperature.

Use your imagination to create your own clay cooker desserts using fresh seasonal fruits. The recipes that follow will suggest the array of possibilities in the mouth-watering world of clay cooker desserts.

Makes 6 to 8 servings

Carrot Pineapple Cake

2   eggs
1   cup (250 mL) sugar
1   teaspoon (5 mL) vanilla
1½   cups (375 mL) all-purpose
     flour
1   teaspoon (5 mL) baking
     powder
1   teaspoon (5 mL) baking soda
1   teaspoon (5 mL) ground
     cinnamon
½   teaspoon (2 mL) salt
¾   cup (180 mL) vegetable oil
1   small can (8 ounces or 225 g)
     crushed pineapple, drained
1   cup (250 mL) pared, finely
     shredded carrots
½   cup (125 mL) finely chopped
     walnuts
     Cream Cheese Icing (recipe
     follows)

Although most clay cooker cakes can be cut and served from the pot in which they baked, here is one you will want to turn out and frost with the tart cream cheese icing everyone loves.

1. Soak top and bottom of 3¼-quart (3.25 L) clay cooker in water about 15 minutes; drain. Pat dry and grease bottom and sides of cooker. Line cooker with parchment paper cut to fit bottom only.

2. Beat eggs, sugar, and vanilla in large mixer bowl until thick. Mix flour, baking powder, baking soda, cinnamon and salt. Beat flour mixture alternately with oil into egg mixture, beating until smooth after each addition.

3. Stir in pineapple, carrots and walnuts. Spread batter in cooker.

4. Place covered cooker in cold oven. Set oven at 350°F (180°C). Bake until wooden pick inserted in center comes out clean, about 1 hour.

5. Let cooker stand on wire rack about 10 minutes; invert cake carefully onto rack. Let stand until completely cooled.

6. Make Cream Cheese Icing.

7. Spread sides and top of cake with icing. Slice or cut into squares or bars.

Cream Cheese Icing

1   small package (3 ounces or
     85 g) cream cheese, room
     temperature
¼   cup (60 mL) butter or
     margarine, room
     temperature
1   teaspoon (5 mL) lemon juice
½   teaspoon (2 mL) vanilla
2   cups (500 mL) powdered sugar

1. Beat cream cheese, butter, lemon juice and vanilla in large mixer bowl until smooth and fluffy.

2. Beat in powdered sugar gradually; beat until icing is proper consistency for spreading.

Makes 6 to 8 servings

Date-Nut Pudding

¾   cup (180 mL) all-purpose flour
1½   teaspoons (7 mL) baking
     powder
½   teaspoon (2 mL) salt
1½   cups (375 mL) chopped pitted
     dates

Easy to make and quick to put together, this is a pleasing dessert to serve warm on a winter evening before a blazing fire.

1. Soak top and bottom of 2-quart (2 L) clay cooker in water about 15 minutes; drain. Pat dry and grease bottom and sides of cooker.

DATE-NUT PUDDING, continued

3/4 cup (180 mL) coarsely chopped
 pecans or walnuts
3 eggs
3/4 cup (180 mL) sugar
2 tablespoons (30 mL) melted
 butter or margarine
 Whipped cream

2. Mix flour, baking powder and salt. Add dates and nuts; coat with flour mixture.

3. Beat eggs in large mixer bowl until blended. Beat in sugar gradually; beat until thick and pale. Add date mixture and butter; mix well. Spread batter in cooker.

4. Place covered cooker in cold oven. Set oven at 350°F (180°C). Bake until top is brown, 45 to 50 minutes.

5. Cut warm pudding into bars or squares; serve with whipped cream.

Makes 6 to 8 servings

Graham Cracker Cake

1 3/4 cups (430 mL) fine graham
 cracker crumbs
1 cup (250 mL) sugar
1/3 cup (80 mL) all-purpose flour
2 teaspoons (10 mL) baking
 powder
2 eggs
1/2 cup (125 mL) butter or
 margarine, room
 temperature
1 cup (250 mL) milk
1 teaspoon (5 mL) vanilla
3/4 cup (180 mL) finely chopped
 walnuts
 Cinnamon Syrup (recipe
 follows)

A warm cinnamon syrup poured over this nut-rich cake gives it an elegant glaze and moist texture. The cake is simplicity itself — a certain success dessert for a beginning cook.

1. Soak top and bottom of 3 1/4-quart (3.25 L) clay cooker in water about 15 minutes; drain. Pat dry and grease bottom and sides of cooker. Line with parchment paper cut to fit bottom only.

2. Combine graham cracker crumbs, sugar, flour and baking powder in large mixer bowl. Add eggs, butter, milk and vanilla. Mix until combined; beat on medium speed until thoroughly blended. Fold in walnuts. Spread batter in cooker.

3. Place covered cooker in cold oven. Set oven at 350°F (180°C). Bake until wooden pick inserted in center comes out clean. 55 to 60 minutes.

4. While cake is baking, make Cinnamon Syrup.

5. Pierce all over surface of warm cake with fork. Pour Cinnamon Syrup slowly over cake. Let stand 15 minutes or longer to allow syrup to soak in. Serve warm.

Cinnamon Syrup

1/2 cup (125 mL) sugar
1/2 teaspoon (2 mL) ground
 cinnamon
1/2 cup (125 mL) whipping cream
1/4 cup (60 mL) butter or
 margarine

1. Mix sugar and cinnamon in small saucepan; add cream and butter. Cook and stir over medium-high heat until boiling; boil 1 minute.

2. Keep syrup warm until ready to use.

DESSERTS

Makes 6 to 8 servings

Deep-Dish Peach Pie

1 **cup (250 mL) sugar**
2 **tablespoons (30 mL) flour**
1/4 **teaspoon (1 mL) ground nutmeg**
1/8 **teaspoon (0.5 mL) salt**
8 **medium peaches (2½ to 3 pounds or 1125 to 1350 g), peeled, sliced**
1 **teaspoon (5 mL) grated lemon rind**
1/4 **teaspoon (1 mL) almond extract**
1/4 **cup (60 mL) butter or margarine**
Cookie Crust (recipe follows)

The crust of this luscious fresh peach pie has the richness of a well made Scottish shortbread cookie.

1. Soak top and bottom of 3¼-quart (3.25 L) clay cooker in water about 15 minutes; drain.

2. Mix sugar, flour, nutmeg and salt in large bowl. Add peaches; combine gently. Fold in lemon rind and almond extract. Spread peach mixture in cooker. Dot with butter.

3. Make Cookie Crust.

4. Roll pastry on floured surface into shape a little larger than upper edge of cooker. Place pastry over peaches, turning edges under and pressing firmly against cooker with fork. Pierce or slit pastry in several places to allow steam to escape.

5. Place covered cooker in cold oven. Set oven at 450°F (230°C). Bake until peaches are tender and crust is brown, 40 to 45 minutes. Serve warm.

Cookie Crust

1¼ **cups (310 mL) all-purpose flour**
2 **tablespoons (30 mL) sugar**
1½ **teaspoons (7 mL) baking powder**
1/4 **teaspoon (1 mL) salt**
3 **tablespoons (45 mL) cold butter or margarine**
1/2 **cup (125 mL) whipping cream**

1. Mix flour, sugar, baking powder and salt in medium bowl. Cut in butter until mixture forms fine crumbs.

2. Stir in cream gradually. Shape dough into ball. Knead lightly on floured surface until smooth, 30 to 45 seconds.

Makes 4 to 6 servings

Apple, Date and Pecan Pudding

4 **medium tart apples, pared, cored, diced**
3/4 **cup (180 mL) sugar**
1/2 **cup (125 mL) chopped pecans**
1/2 **cup (125 mL) cut pitted dates**
2 **tablespoons (30 mL) flour**
1 **teaspoon (5 mL) baking powder**
1/8 **teaspoon (0.5 mL) salt**
1/8 **teaspoon (0.5 mL) ground nutmeg**

Here is an enticing fruit and nut dessert to serve warm from the oven, with whipped cream or frosty scoops of vanilla ice cream.

1. Soak top and bottom of 2-quart (2 L) clay cooker in water about 15 minutes; drain and pat dry.

2. Combine apples, sugar, pecans and dates. Mix flour, baking powder, salt and nutmeg; fold into apple mixture. Add egg; mix lightly with fork just until blended.

146

APPLE, DATE AND PECAN PUDDING, continued

1   egg
2   tablespoons (30 mL) melted
      butter or margarine
    Whipped cream or vanilla ice
      cream

3. Brush bottom and sides of cooker with butter. Spread apple mixture in cooker.

4. Place covered cooker in cold oven. Set oven at 450°F (230°C). Bake until apples are tender, about 45 minutes. Remove cover; bake until top is golden, about 5 minutes. Serve hot with whipped cream or ice cream.

Makes 1 cake

Brown Sugar Pound Cake

1   cup (250 mL) butter or
      margarine, room
      temperature
1   cup (250 mL) packed light
      brown sugar
1   teaspoon (5 mL) vanilla
4   eggs
1³/₄ cups (430 mL) all-purpose
      flour
¹/₂ teaspoon (2 mL) baking
      powder
¹/₄ teaspoon (1 mL) salt

This fine-textured pound cake has a buttery toffee flavor. Thin slices are good with afternoon tea or coffee — or for dessert with sliced strawberries.

1. Soak top and bottom of loaf-shaped, 5¹/₂-cup (1375 mL) clay cooker in water about 15 minutes; drain. Pat dry and grease bottom and sides of cooker. Line cooker with parchment paper cut to fit bottom only.

2. Beat butter, brown sugar and vanilla in large mixer bowl until light and fluffy. Beat in eggs, one at a time, beating well after each addition. Mix flour, baking powder and salt; beat into egg mixture gradually. Spread batter in cooker.

3. Place covered cooker in cold oven. Set oven at 375°F (190°C). Bake until wooden pick inserted in center comes out clean, about 1 hour.

4. Let cooker stand on wire rack about 5 minutes. Remove cake from cooker; cool on rack. Cut into ¹/₂-inch (1.5 cm) slices.

Makes 6 to 8 servings

Creamy Rice Pudding

2   tablespoons (30 mL) melted
      butter or margarine
¹/₂ cup (125 mL) uncooked long-
      grain rice
¹/₂ cup (125 mL) sugar
¹/₂ teaspoon (2 mL) salt
¹/₂ teaspoon (2 mL) ground
      nutmeg
1   quart (1 L) milk
2   cups (500 mL) half-and-half
2   teaspoons (10 mL) vanilla
³/₄ cup (180 mL) dark raisins
    Cream

Remember how your grandmother used to make rice pudding, simmering it for hours in rich milk with plump raisins! This clay cooker version duplicates the sweet tenderness of the rice, and long slow baking in clay gives the pudding a tempting caramel color.

1. Soak top and bottom of 3¹/₄-quart (3.25 L) clay cooker in water about 15 minutes; drain. Pat dry and brush bottom and sides of cooker with butter.

2. Combine rice, sugar, salt, nutmeg, milk, half-and-half and vanilla in cooker.

3. Place covered cooker in cold oven. Set oven at 350°F (180°C). Bake 1 hour; stir in raisins. Bake covered, stirring once or twice in the first hour, until pudding is crusty, about 2 hours. Remove cover; bake until top is brown, 8 to 10 minutes. Serve warm or cold; pour cream over each serving.

Makes 4 servings

Poached Pears in Butter-Rum Sauce

4 medium pears
1/4 teaspoon (1 mL) ground mace or nutmeg
1/2 cup (125 mL) packed brown sugar
1/4 cup (60 mL) cold butter, cut into small pieces
1/4 cup (60 mL) rum
1/2 cup (125 mL) whipping cream

For this dessert select fat, round winter pears such as the Anjou or Comice varieties. For best baking, Anjou pears can be slightly underripe.

1. Soak top and bottom of square 2-quart (2 L) clay cooker in water about 15 minutes; drain.

2. Pare pears, leaving stems on. Carefully remove cores from bottoms, leaving tops intact. Stand pears upright in cooker. Sprinkle with mace; sprinkle with brown sugar. Dot with butter. Pour in rum.

3. Place covered cooker in cold oven. Set oven at 450°F (230°C). Bake until pears are tender, 45 to 50 minutes. Remove pears to warm individual serving bowls; keep warm.

4. Pour cooking liquid into 1 1/2-quart (1.5 L) saucepan. Stir in cream. Heat to boiling; boil, stirring occasionally, until sauce is reduced by about a third and slightly thickened. Pour over pears. Serve hot.

Makes 6 servings

Mom's Cherry Pudding

1 can (1 pound or 450 g) pitted sour red cherries
1 cup (250 mL) sugar
4 tablespoons (60 mL) butter or margarine, room temperature
1/2 teaspoon (2 mL) vanilla
1 cup (250 mL) all-purpose flour
1 teaspoon (5 mL) baking powder
1/2 cup (125 mL) milk
Cream or vanilla ice cream

When you put this colorful tart cherry dessert together, the cakelike batter is on the bottom and cherries and their syrup are on top. But as the pudding bakes, the fruit and juices go to the bottom to form a juicy crimson layer. This is a dessert that is at its best moments out of the oven.

1. Soak top and bottom of 2-quart (2 L) clay cooker in water about 15 minutes; drain.

2. Drain cherries; reserve 3/4 cup (180 mL) of the juice. Cook juice and 1/2 cup (125 mL) of the sugar, stirring constantly, until sugar dissolves.

3. Cream 3 tablespoons (45 mL) of the butter, the vanilla and remaining sugar in large mixer bowl. Mix flour and baking powder. Stir flour mixture alternately with milk into butter mixture, mixing just until smooth after each addition.

4. Melt remaining butter. Pat dry and brush bottom and sides of cooker with butter. Spread batter in cooker. Top with drained cherries in even layer. Pour cherry syrup over cherries.

5. Place covered cooker in cold oven. Set oven at 450°F (230°C). Bake until top is golden and wooden pick inserted in center comes out clean, about 45 minutes. Remove cover; bake until top is brown, about 5 minutes. Serve hot, with cream or ice cream.

Indian Pudding

Makes 6 to 8 servings

2   tablespoons (30 mL) melted
      butter or margarine
1   quart (1 L) milk
1/3   cup (80 mL) light molasses
1/2   cup (125 mL) sugar
1/4   cup (60 mL) yellow cornmeal
2   eggs, lightly beaten
2   tablespoons (30 mL) butter or
      margarine, room
      temperature
1/2   teaspoon (2 mL) ground
      cinnamon
1/4   teaspoon (1 mL) ground ginger
      Pinch salt
      Vanilla ice cream or whipped
      cream

This style of pudding, thickened with cornmeal and flavored with spices and molasses, is a New England favorite with a history going back to Colonial times. The spicing and consistency are reminiscent of pumpkin pie.

1. Soak top and bottom of 2-quart (2 L) cooker in water about 15 minutes; drain. Brush inside surfaces of bottom of cooker with melted butter.

2. Scald milk in a heavy 2-quart (2 L) saucepan. Stir in molasses, sugar and cornmeal. Heat to boiling; reduce heat. Simmer, stirring occasionally, until thick, about 20 minutes; remove from heat.

3. Beat a little of the hot cornmeal mixture into eggs in bowl. Stir egg mixture into cornmeal mixture; whisk in room temperature butter, the cinnamon, ginger and salt. Pour into cooker.

4. Place covered cooker in cold oven. Set oven at 325°F (160°C). Bake until pudding is firm and edges brown, 2¼ to 2½ hours. Remove cover; bake 5 to 10 minutes.

5. Let stand at least 15 minutes. Serve warm with ice cream or whipped cream.

Blueberry Buckle

Makes 6 servings

      Crumble Topping (recipe
      follows)
1/4   cup (60 mL) butter or
      margarine, room
      temperature
1/2   cup (125 mL) sugar
1   egg
1   teaspoon (5 mL) vanilla
1   cup (250 mL) all-purpose flour
1   teaspoon (5 mL) baking
      powder
1/4   teaspoon (1 mL) salt
1/3   cup (80 mL) milk
1   tablespoon (15 mL) melted
      butter or margarine
2   cups (500 mL) fresh
      blueberries, rinsed, stemmed
      Whipped cream or ice cream, if
      desired

Some of the most curiously named fruit puddings have New England origins. Consider apple slump, cranberry grunt and this crumble-topped Blueberry Buckle!

1. Make Crumble Topping.

2. Soak top and bottom of 2-quart (2 L) clay cooker in water about 15 minutes; drain.

3. While cooker is soaking, cream ¼ cup (60 mL) butter and the sugar in large mixer bowl. Beat in egg and vanilla. Mix flour, baking powder and salt. Beat in flour mixture alternately with milk, beating until smooth after each addition.

4. Pat dry and brush bottom and sides of cooker with melted butter. Spread batter in cooker. Sprinkle with blueberries. Spoon Crumble Topping over berries.

BLUEBERRY BUCKLE, continued

5. Place covered cooker in cold oven. Set oven at 450°F (230°C). Bake until wooden pick inserted in center comes out clean, about 40 minutes. Remove cover, bake until brown, about 5 minutes.

6. Serve warm, with whipped cream or ice cream, if desired.

Crumble Topping

1/2 cup (125 mL) sugar	1. Mix sugar, flour and spices. Cut in butter until mixture forms coarse crumbs.
1/4 cup (60 mL) all-purpose flour	
1/2 teaspoon (2 mL) ground cinnamon	
1/8 teaspoon (0.5 mL) ground nutmeg	
1/4 cup (60 mL) butter or margarine	

Makes 6 servings

Gooey Chocolate Pudding

1 cup (250 mL) all-purpose flour
2/3 cup (160 mL) granulated sugar
2 tablespoons (30 mL) unsweetened cocoa
2 teaspoons (10 mL) baking powder
1/2 teaspoon (2 mL) salt
1/2 cup (125 mL) milk
1/2 cup (125 mL) chopped walnuts
2 tablespoons (30 mL) melted butter or margarine
1 teaspoon (5 mL) vanilla
Brown Sugar Topping (recipe follows)
1 cup (250 mL) boiling water
Whipped cream

In a sense this is a hot-fudge version of the preceding cherry pudding — a chocolate-nut pudding that makes it's own dark chocolate sauce.

1. Soak top and bottom of 3 1/4-quart (3.25 L) clay cooker in water about 15 minutes; drain. Pat dry and grease inside bottom and sides of cooker.

2. Mix flour, sugar, cocoa, baking powder and salt in large bowl. Add milk, walnuts, butter and vanilla; stir until blended. Spread in cooker.

3. Make Brown Sugar Topping.

4. Sprinkle Brown Sugar Topping over batter. Pour in boiling water without stirring.

5. Place covered cooker in cold oven. Set oven at 375°F (190°C). Bake until top is firm, about 1 hour. Serve pudding hot, with whipped cream.

Brown Sugar Topping

1/2 cup (125 mL) packed brown sugar	1. Mix all ingredients.
1/4 cup (60 mL) granulated sugar	
3 tablespoons (45 mL) unsweetened cocoa	
1/4 teaspoon (1 mL) salt	
1 teaspoon (5 mL) vanilla	

Makes 6 servings

Deep-Dish Brown Sugar Apple Pie

1   **cup (250 mL) packed brown sugar**
2   **tablespoons (30 mL) flour**
1/8   **teaspoon (0.5 mL) salt**
1   **teaspoon (5 mL) ground cinnamon**
1   **teaspoon (5 mL) grated lemon rind**
1/4   **teaspoon (1 mL) ground mace or nutmeg**
6   **medium tart apples, pared, cored, thinly sliced (about 8 cups or 2 L)**
2   **tablespoons (30 mL) butter or margarine**
    Flaky Pastry (recipe follows)

Clay cooking gives this deep-dish apple pie a wonderfully old-fashioned flavor, and the traditional top crust is as crisp and flaky as anyone could wish.

1. Soak top and bottom of square 2-quart (2 L) clay cooker in water about 15 minutes; drain.

2. Mix brown sugar, flour, salt, cinnamon, lemon rind and mace in large bowl. Add sliced apples; combine gently. Spread apple mixture in cooker. Dot with butter.

3. Make Flaky Pastry.

4. Roll pastry on floured surface into a square a little larger than upper edge of cooker. Place pastry over apples, turning edges under and pressing firmly against cooker with fork. Slit pastry in several places to allow steam to escape.

5. Place covered cooker in cold oven. Set oven at 450°F (230°C). Bake until apples are tender and crust is brown, about 1 hour. If necessary, remove cover and bake until crust is brown, about 5 minutes. Serve warm or at room temperature; cut into squares.

Flaky Pastry

1   **cup (250 mL) all-purpose flour**
1   **tablespoon (15 mL) powdered sugar**
1/4   **cup (60 mL) firm butter or margarine**
1   **tablespoon (15 mL) lard**
1 1/2 **to 2 tablespoons (22 to 30 mL) cold water**

1. Mix flour and powdered sugar. Cut in butter and lard until mixture forms coarse crumbs. Stir in cold water until dough cleans side of bowl.

2. Shape dough into ball.

Makes 4 servings

Caramel-Nut Baked Apples

4   **large baking apples**
1/3   **cup (80 mL) packed brown sugar**
1   **tablespoon (15 mL) butter or margarine, room temperature**
1   **teaspoon (5 mL) grated lemon rind**
1/4   **cup (60 mL) finely chopped pecans**
    Whipped cream, if desired

Baked apples are a fairly light dessert for an autumn supper. Filling them with a mixture of brown sugar, butter, lemon rind and chopped pecans makes them special.

1. Soak top and bottom of square 2-quart (2 L) clay cooker in water about 15 minutes; drain.

2. Core apples from stem end without cutting through to bottom. Pare upper quarter of each apple.

(Continued on page 154)

CARMEL-NUT BAKED APPLES, continued

3. Mix brown sugar, butter and lemon rind until smooth; stir in pecans. Fill apples with pecan mixture. Place apples in cooker.

4. Place covered cooker in cold oven. Set oven at 450°F (230°C). Bake until apples are tender, 40 to 45 minutes. Serve hot. Top with whipped cream, if desired.

Old-Fashioned Spiced Applesauce

Makes about 3 cups (750 mL)

6   medium tart apples, cored, cut
        into chunks
¼   cup (60 mL) sugar
1   tablespoon (15 mL) lemon
        juice
½   teaspoon (2 mL) grated lemon
        rind
1   piece cinnamon stick, 2 inches
        (5 cm) long
¼   teaspoon (1 mL) ground
        nutmeg
⅛   teaspoon (0.5 mL) ground
        allspice

Delicious either as a simple dessert with cookies or as a side dish for German foods, such as Sauerbraten (see Index for page number), this applesauce can be served either warm or chilled.

1. Soak top and bottom of 2-quart (2 L) clay cooker in water about 15 minutes; drain.

2. Combine all ingredients in cooker.

3. Place covered cooker in cold oven. Set oven at 425°F (220°C). Bake, stirring once or twice, until apples are very tender, about 45 minutes. Taste and add sugar, if needed. Serve warm or cold.

Lemon Caramel Custard

Makes 6 to 8 servings

2   tablespoons (30 mL) melted
        butter or margarine
½   cup (125 mL) packed dark
        brown sugar
3½   cups (875 mL) milk
1   cup (250 mL) whipping cream
5   eggs
5   egg yolks
¾   cup (180 mL) granulated sugar
2   tablespoons (30 mL) lemon
        juice
1   teaspoon (5 mL) grated lemon
        rind
1   teaspoon (5 mL) vanilla

A generous layer of brown sugar in the bottom of the clay cooker gives this silken lemon custard a caramel glaze.

1. Soak top and bottom of 3¼-quart (3.25 L) clay cooker in water about 15 minutes; drain.

2. Pat dry and brush bottom and sides of cooker with butter. Pat brown sugar over bottom and 1 inch (2.5 cm) up sides of cooker.

3. Scald milk and cream. Beat eggs, egg yolks and sugar in large mixer bowl until light and frothy. Pour milk mixture in slow steady stream into eggs, stirring constantly. Stir in lemon juice, rind and vanilla. Pour into cooker.

4. Place covered cooker in cold oven. Set oven at 325°F (160°C). Bake until small knife inserted in center comes out clean, about 1 hour.

5. Let custard stand uncovered at room temperature about 1 hour. Refrigerate until cold, 3 to 4 hours. Invert custard into a serving bowl.

Lemon-Pineapple Soufflé in Clay

Makes 6 servings

1   can (20 ounces or 550 g)
         crushed pineapple
3   tablespoons (45 mL) melted
         butter or margarine
4   eggs, separated
1/2 cup (125 mL) sugar
1/4 cup (60 mL) all-purpose flour
1   lemon
3/4 cup (180 mL) milk
1/8 teaspoon (0.5 mL) cream of
         tartar
     Whipped cream, if desired

Part soufflé, part pudding, this tart fruit dessert has a puffy topping over a layer of fruit custard. Like all soufflés, it is at its best served directly from the oven, for the egg white-leavened pouf gradually deflates as it cools.

1. Soak top and bottom of square 2-quart (2 L) clay cooker in water about 15 minutes; drain.

2. Drain pineapple; reserve 3/4 cup (180 mL) of the liquid.

3. Brush inside surfaces of bottom of cooker with 1 tablespoon (15 mL) of the butter. Spread drained pineapple evenly in bottom of cooker. Beat egg yolks in large mixer bowl until thick; mix in 6 tablespoons (90 mL) sugar and the flour until smooth. Grate lemon rind; squeeze juice. Mix lemon rind and juice, reserved pineapple liquid, the milk and remaining butter into egg mixture.

4. Clean mixer bowl and beaters. Beat egg whites until foamy. Add cream of tartar; beat until stiff but not dry peaks form. Beat in remaining sugar gradually; beat until egg whites are stiff and glossy. Fold egg whites into egg yolk mixture. Spread evenly over pineapple.

5. Place covered cooker in cold oven. Set oven at 450°F (230°C). Bake until top browns, about 45 minutes. Serve immediately. Top with whipped cream, if desired.

Cranberry Apple Betty

Makes 6 servings

1   cup (250 mL) all-purpose flour
1/2 cup (125 mL) sugar
1/4 teaspoon (1 mL) ground
         nutmeg
1/2 cup (125 mL) cold butter or
         margarine
1/4 cup (60 mL) shredded Cheddar
         cheese
2   medium tart cooking apples,
         pared, cored, thinly sliced
1   can (16 ounces or 450 g)
         whole-berry cranberry sauce
1/4 cup (60 mL) sugar
2   teaspoons (10 mL) quick-
         cooking tapioca
1/2 teaspoon (2 mL) grated lemon
         rind
     Sour cream, if desired

Canned whole cranberry sauce and sliced fresh apples topped with a crusty cheese-flecked topping make an appealing tart-sweet dessert for a cold weather supper.

1. Soak top and bottom of 2-quart (2 L) clay cooker in water about 15 minutes; drain.

2. Mix flour, 1/2 cup (125 mL) sugar and the nutmeg. Cut in butter until mixture forms coarse crumbs; stir in cheese.

3. Combine apples, cranberry sauce, 1/4 cup (60 mL) sugar, the tapioca and lemon rind in cooker. Cover with butter mixture.

4. Place covered cooker in cold oven. Set oven at 475°F (250°C). Bake until apples are tender and sauce bubbles, about 35 minutes. Remove cover; bake until topping is brown and crisp, 3 to 5 minutes.

5. Serve warm. Top with sour cream, if desired.

Rhubarb Crumble

Makes 4 to 6 servings

1   cup (250 mL) all-purpose flour
1/2 cup (125 mL) packed brown sugar
1/2 cup (125 mL) cold butter or margarine
1   pound (450 g) fresh rhubarb, cut into 1/2-inch (1.5 cm) slices (about 4 cups or 1 L)
3/4 cup (180 mL) granulated sugar
2   teaspoons (10 mL) quick-cooking tapioca
1/2 teaspoon (2 mL) ground cinnamon
1/8 teaspoon (0.5 mL) ground nutmeg
    Whipped cream, if desired

If you have more than one clay cooker, you can bake this fresh rhubarb dessert at the same time you are cooking a main dish such as chicken, roast pork or ham.

1. Soak top and bottom of 2-quart (2 L) clay cooker in water about 15 minutes; drain.

2. Mix flour and brown sugar. Cut in butter until mixture forms coarse crumbs.

3. Combine rhubarb, granulated sugar, tapioca, cinnamon and nutmeg in cooker. Cover with brown sugar mixture.

4. Place covered cooker in cold oven. Set oven at 475°F (250°C). Bake until rhubarb is tender and sauce is bubbly, about 35 minutes. Remove cover; bake until topping is brown and crisp, 3 to 5 minutes.

5. Serve warm, topped with whipped cream, if desired.

Toffee Cake

Makes 8 servings

2 3/4 cups (680 mL) all-purpose flour
2   cups (500 mL) packed brown sugar
1   tablespoon (15 mL) baking powder
1   teaspoon (5 mL) salt
3/4 cup (180 mL) butter or margarine
1   cup (250 mL) milk
2   teaspoons (10 mL) vanilla
2   eggs
3   tablespoons (45 mL) butter or margarine
1/2 cup (125 mL) chopped pecans
1/3 cup (80 mL) chocolate shot

A baked-on chocolate-nut topping gives this brown sugar cake a crisp self-frosting. Cut into generous chunks, it will be a hit at a picnic or potluck.

1. Soak top and bottom of 3 1/4-quart (3.25 L) clay cooker in water about 15 minutes; drain. Pat dry and grease bottom and sides of cooker. Line cooker with parchment paper cut to fit bottom only.

2. Mix flour, brown sugar, baking powder and salt in large mixer bowl. Cut in 3/4 cup (180 mL) butter until mixture forms fine crumbs; remove and reserve 1 cup (250 mL) of the flour mixture.

3. Add milk and vanilla to remaining flour mixture in bowl; mix until blended. Beat in eggs, one at a time, beating until smooth after each addition. Spread batter in cooker.

4. Cut 3 tablespoons (45 mL) butter into reserved flour mixture; stir in nuts and chocolate shot. Sprinkle evenly over batter.

5. Place covered cooker in cold oven. Set oven at 350°F (180°C). Bake until wooden pick inserted in center comes out clean, about 1 1/2 to 1 3/4 hours. Cool in cooker on wire rack. Cut into bars or squares.

Index